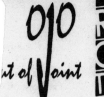

The Royal Court Theatre and Out of Joint,
in association with Bristol Old Vic and
Leicester Haymarket Theatre
present

The Break of Day

by Timberlake Wertenbaker

ff

faber and faber
LONDON · BOSTON

First performed at the Royal Court Theatre Downstairs 22 November 1995.
First performed at the Leicester Haymarket 26 October 1995.

The Royal Court Theatre is financially assisted by the
Royal Borough of Kensington and Chelsea.
Recipient of a grant from the Theatre Restoration Fund &
from the Foundation for Sport & the Arts.
The Royal Court's Play Development Programme is funded
by the Audrey Skirball-Kenis Theatre.
The Royal Court Registered Charity Number 231242
Out of Joint Registered Charity Number 1033059

firstcall
TICKETS · 24 HOURS
0171 420 0100

THE
ARTS
COUNCIL
OF ENGLAND

First published in 1995
by Faber and Faber Limited
3 Queen Square London WC1N 3AU
in association with the Royal Court Theatre
Sloane Square London SW1N 8AS

Printed in England by Clays Ltd, St Ives plc

A CIP record for this book
is available from the British Library

ISBN 0-571-15383-6

The English Stage Company at the Royal Court Theatre

The English Stage Company was formed to bring serious writing back to the stage. The Court's first Artistic Director, George Devine, wanted to create a vital and popular theatre. He encouraged new writing that explored subjects drawn from contemporary life as well as pursuing European plays and forgotten classics. When John Osbornes **Look Back in Anger** was first produced in 1956, it forced British Theatre into the modern age. But, the Court was much more than a home for 'Angry Young Men' illustrated by a repertoire that stretched from Brecht to Ionesco, by way of J P Sartre, Marguerite Duras, Wedekind and Beckett.

The ambition was to discover new work which was challenging, innovative and also of the highest quality, underpinned by the desire to discover a truly contemporary style of presentation. Early Court writers included Arnold Wesker, John Arden, David Storey, Ann Jellicoe, N F Simpson and Edward Bond. They were followed by a generation of writers led by David Hare and Howard Brenton, and in more recent years, celebrated house writers have included Caryl Churchill, Timberlake Wertenbaker, Robert Holman and Jim Cartwright. Many of their plays are now regarded as modern classics.

In line with the policy of nurturing new writing, the Theatre Upstairs has mainly been seen as a place for exploration and experiment, where writers learn and develop their skills. Anne Devlin, Andrea Dunbar, Sarah Daniels, Jim Cartwright, Clare McIntyre, Winsome Pinnock, and more recently Martin Crimp and Phyllis Nagy have benefited from this process. Theatre Upstairs productions have regularly transferred to the Theatre Downstairs, as with Ariel Dorfman's **Death and the Maiden**, and this autumn Sebastian Barry's **The Steward of Christendom**, a co-production with *Out of Joint*. This was part of a major season of plays by writers new to the Royal Court, many of them first plays, produced in association with the Royal National Theatre Studio with sponsorship from the Jerwood Foundation. The writers included Joe Penhall, Nick Grosso, Judy Upton, Sarah Kane, Michael Wynne, Judith Johnson and James Stock.

1992-1995 have been record-breaking years at the box-office with capacity houses for productions of **Faith Healer**, **Death and the Maiden**, **Six Degrees of Separation**, **King Lear**, **Oleanna**, **Hysteria**, **Cavalcaders, The Kitchen, The Queen & I, The Libertine**, **Simpatico** and **Mojo**.

Death and the Maiden and **Six Degrees of Separation** won the Olivier Award for Best Play in 1992 and 1993 respectively. **Hysteria** won 1994's Olivier Award for Best Comedy, and also the Writer's Guild Award for Best West End Play. **My Night with Reg** won the 1994 Writer's Guild Award for Best Fringe Play, the Evening Standard Award for Best Comedy, and Best Comedy in this year's Olivier Awards. Jonathan Harvey won the 1994 Evening Standard Drama Award for Most Promising Playwright, for **Babies**. Sebastian Barry won the 1995 Writers' Guild Award for Best Fringe Play for **The Steward of Christendom**, Jez Butterworth was named *New Writer of the Year* for **Mojo** by the Writers' Guild and Phyllis Nagy won the Writers' Guild Award for Best Regional Play for **Disappeared**. The Royal Court has just been awarded the 1*995 Prudential Award for Excellence and Innovation in Theatre.*

After nearly four decades, the Royal Court's aims remain consistent with those established by George Devine. The Royal Court Theatre is still a major focus in the country for the production of new work. Scores of plays first seen in Sloane Square are now part of the national and internationall dramatic repertoire.

OJO
Out of Joint

Out of Joint is a theatre company established in 1993 by Max Stafford-Clark and Sonia Friedman to enable new and classic plays to be produced under the best conditions for the stage. Usually two plays, thematically linked, are toured in repertoire to theatres nationally and internationally.

The name Out of Joint indicates the philosophy of the company; the point of departure is the work pioneered by Joint Stock in the 1970s and to a certain extent carried on during Max Stafford-Clark's tenure of the Royal Court in the 80s and early 90s.

Photo: John Haynes

Donal McCann in Sebastian Barry's
The Steward of Christendom.

Out of Joint's inaugural production was a new play **The Queen and I by** Sue Townsend's, paired with a revival of **Road** by Jim Cartwright. The two productions toured the country for ten weeks before settling at the Royal Court. **The Queen and I** was nominated for a *Martini/TMA Award for Best Touring Production,* transferred to the West End, and has just completed its' second national tour. This was followed by **The Libertine,** an account of The Earl of Rochester's extraordinary life, by Stephen Jeffreys. This toured in repertoire with the Restoration classic **The Man of Mode.** In March '95, the company

toured Sebastian Barry's **The Steward of Christendom**. The play sold out at the Royal Court, at the Liverpool Everyman and at the Gate Theatre in Dublin. It also won the Best Drama Award at the Brighton Festival, and Sebastian Barry has just received a Writers' Guild Award for Best Fringe Play. Following its recent return to the Royal Court Downstairs, **The Steward of Christendom** tours to Sydney, Adelaide, Wellington and Dublin. **The Break of Day**, sees Out of Joint joining forces once more wth the Royal Court to produce this new play by Timberlake Wertenbaker. **The Break of Day** will tour the UK in repertoire with Chekhov's classic, **Three Sisters**, which following its' international tour will also play at the Lyric Hammersmith.

Further plans include new plays by Sebastian Barry, Caryl Churchill and April de Angelis, and a new Australian version of **The Queen and I**, entitled **The Royals Down Under** which will tour Australia from June 1995.

Production co-producers:
The Queen and I
Out of Joint, The Royal Court Theatre and the Haymarket Theatre Leicester.
Road
Out of Joint and The Royal Court Theatre
The Libertine &
The Man of Mode
Out of Joint and The Royal Court Theatre
The Steward of Christendom
Out of Joint and The Royal Court
Three Sisters
Out of Joint, The Royal Court Theatre , in association with Bristol Old Vic and Leicester Haymarket Theatre.

For Out of Joint   20/24 Eden Grove
                           London N7 8ED
                           Tel 0171-609-0207

Director   **Max Stafford-Clark**
Producer   **Sonia Friedman**
Assistant Director   **Guy Retallack**
Production Managers   **Iain Gillie**
                           Jerry Donaldson
Company Manager   **Rob Young**
Administrative Assistant   **Sally Pearson**
Literary Adviser   **Philip Kingston**
Press & Marketing   **Chapman Duncan**
                           Associates
                           0171- 242 -1882

Royal Court Theatre to Survive

The Royal Court theatre has just received the news that it has been awarded a much needed grant of just under £16 million from the Arts Council Lottery Fund, to refurbish and develop its unique property in Sloane Square, ensuring the theatre's survival well into the next century.

The application to the Arts Council for this award would not have been possible without the efforts and support of the recent *Olivier Appeal* which enabled the Royal Court to begin repairs and improvements to the building. We would like to say a very big thank you to all of those people involved with the *Olivier Appeal* and hope that they will continue to support us in this new and exciting phase in the Royal Court's history, as we complete the refurbishment with the new Arts Council funding.

As Stephen Daldry, Artistic Director states:
'The theatre is in such a terrible physical state at the moment that without this funding we would not have been able to survive more than about 18 months. This would have meant the end of this unique and wonderful playhouse. Now we can face the future with confidence and carry on the work of promoting new plays and playwrights'

Development plans include a complete renovation of the theatre - without losing any of its unique charm and relaxed atmosphere. Access will be improved, including facilities for wheelchairs. Theatre-goers will enjoy vastly better conditions including improved seating in the auditorium and larger and better equipped refreshment areas. Funds have also been provided for a feasibility study into a new performance space for the Royal Court Young People's Theatre enabling it to continue its important work.

The Royal Court still faces a huge task, to raise the additional partnership funding of £5 million necessary to secure the Arts Council's funding.

With your help we are confident of meeting our target. A tour of the theatre, including its more picturesque parts, can be arranged by ringing *Josephine Campbell* on *0171 730 5174.* If you would like to help with an event or a gift please ring *Joyce Hytner*, Development Director on *0171 823 4132.*

'Secure the theatre's future, and take it forward towards the new century. For the health of the whole theatrical life of Britain it is essential that this greatly all-providing theatre we love so much and wish so well continues to prosper'
Laurence Olivier 1988

Photo: Richard Kalina

The Break of Day

by Timberlake Wertenbaker

CAST *in order of appearance*

NINA	Maria Friedman
TESS	Catherine Russell
HUGH	Brian Protheroe
PAUL	Lloyd Hutchinson
APRIL	Anita Dobson
NATASHA	Madlena Nedeva
JAMIE	David Fielder
ROBERT	Nigel Terry
NICK	Barnaby Kay
MARISA	Kate Ashfield
MR HARDACRE	Jerome Willis
MIHAIL	Bernard Gallagher
DOCTOR GLAD	Lloyd Hutchinson
EVA	Madlena Nedeva
BOIAN	James Goode
DOCTOR ATTANASOV	David Fielder
MISTER STATELOV	Jerome Willis
DOCTOR ROMANOVA	Anita Dobson
VICTOR	James Goode

Other characters played by members of the company.

Director	Max Stafford-Clark
Designer	Julian McGowan
Songs	Jeremy Sams
Lighting Designer	Johanna Town
Sound Designer	John A. Leonard
Musical Director	Steven Edis
Dialect Coach	Jeannette Nelson
Company Manager	Rob Young
Deputy Stage Manager	Helen Barratt
Assistant Stage Manager	Nick Marchand
Costume Supervisor	Lisa Shanley
Assistant Director	Guy Retallack
Production Manager	Jerry Donaldson
Production Photographer	John Haynes

TIMBERLAKE WERTENBAKER (writer)

Plays produced at Royal Court include: Three Birds Alighting on a Field (winner Susan Smith Blackburn, Writers' Guild and London Critics' Circle Awards), Our Country's Good (Olivier Play of the Year 1988, played at the Garrick and on Broadway in 1990 where it was nominated for six Tonies and won the New York Drama Critics' Circle Award for Best Foreign Play), The Grace of Mary Traverse (Plays and Players Most Promising Playwright Award 1985), Abels's Sister. Timberlake was resident writer at the Royal Court in 1984/85.

Other plays include: Case to Answer (Soho Poly); New Anatomies (Women's Theatre Group, ICA); The Love of the Nightingale (RSC, winner Eileen Anderson Award 1989).

Translations include work by: Marivaux, Anouilh, Maeterlinck; for the RSC Mnouchkine's Mephisto and Sophocles' Theban Plays; and for ACT San Francisco, Euripides' Hekabe.

Screenplays include: The Children, Do Not Disturb.

KATE ASHFIELD

For the Royal Court: Blasted, Peaches.

Other theatre includes: Three Sisters (Out of Joint tour), The Importance Of Being Earnest (Royal Exchange); A Collier's Friday Night, Bearing Fruit (Hampstead).

Television includes: Prime Suspect, Fist Of Fun, All Or Nothing, No Bananas.

Film: Princess Caraboo.

ANITA DOBSON

Theatre includes:Three Sisters (Out of Joint tour), Eurovision (Vaudeville); Big Night Out (Nottingham Playhouse); Le Bourgeois Gentilhomme (RNT); Kvetch (Garrick); My Lovely...Shayna Maidel (Ambassadors); Rough Crossing (Kings Head); Wild Justice (Stratford East); Budgie (Cambridge); Henry IV Part I, The Caucasian Chalk Circle (Oxford Playhouse); Charley's Aunt (Lyric/Aldwych); Ardele (Queens); A Slight Ache, The Collection, Old Times, Arden of Favisham, Tartuffe, Tambourlane the Great, Macbeth (Glasgow Citizens); Leave Him to Heaven (New London); The Wizard of Oz, The Alchemist, Deeds (Nottingham Playhouse); Side by Side by Sondheim, Pygmalion (Salisbury).

Television includes: Dangerfield, Go Back Out, I'll Be Watching You, Smokescreen, Woof, The Fireboy, Rab C.Nesbitt, The World of Eddie Weary, Eastenders, Up The Elephant And Round The Castle, Partners In Crime, Take The Stage, Nanny, Leave Him To Heaven.

Films include: Beyond Bedlam, Seaview Knights, Need, The Euphoric Scale.

STEVEN EDIS (musical director)

As musical director: Arcadia, Ting tang Mine, Mrs Warren's Profession, Fathers and Sons, Trelawny of the Wells, Rosencrantz and Guildenstern are Dead (RNT); The Blue Angel (arranger & M.D), Measure for Measure (RSC). Other composing and arranging credits: Johnny on a Spot, (RNT); Macbeth (Newbury and world tour); Henry VIII - Diary of a Serial Killer (Natural Theatre Co.), The Music Man (Regents Park); The Sound of Music (West Yorkshire Playhouse), Watch Your Step (Musica Nel Chiostro).

Television includes: Every Silver Lining, Once in a Lifetime, The Disney Christmas Special.

DAVID FIELDER

For the Royal Court: Uganda, Not Quite Jerusalem, Panic.

Other theatre includes: Three Sisters (Out of Joint tour), A Midsummer Night's Dream (Open Air Theatre, Regents Park & tour of India & Sri Lanka); Trafford Tanzi (Lyric, Shaftesbury Avenue); The Choice (Salisbury Playhouse/TMA Award for Best Actor); Anna Karenina (Shared Experience tour); Richard II (Manchester Royal Exchange); King Lear (Talawa Theatre at the Jeanetta Cochrane); Twelfth Night (tour of China, Salisbury Playhouse, Edinburgh Lyceum).

Met Samuel Beckett in Paris and performed a one-man show compiled from 20 pieces of his work called Beginning To End.

As a writer he co-adapted Trilby for Shared Experience Theatre, of which he is an Associate Member.

TV includes: The Naked Civil Servant, Inspector Morse, Spatz, Widows, The Bill, Heart Beat.

Films include: Yanks, Superman III, The Pledge.

MARIA FRIEDMAN

Theatre includes: Maria Friedman - By Special Arrangement (Donmar Warehouse & Whitehall Olivier Award Best Entertainer 1994); April In Paris (Ambassadors); Square Rounds, Sunday In The Park With George, Ghetto (RNT); Merrily We Roll Along (Haymarket Theatre, Leicester); The Day You'll Love Me (Hampstead); By George It's Gershwin (Purcell Rooms); Cavalcade (Chichester Festival); Blondel (Aldwych); Oklahoma (Palace).

Television includes: Me and the Girls, Blues In The Night, Hardy On, Red Dwarf, Heil Honey I'm Home, Casualty, Divorce, Shakers, Black Daisies For The Bride, Frank Stubbs Promotes, The Complete Guide To Relationships, The Ancient Mariner.

Live concert appearances: Queen Elizabeth Hall, Purcell Room, Royal Festival Hall, The Barbican, Royal Albert Hall, Drury Lane, Shaftesbury Avenue, The Playhouse, Edinburgh Concert Hall, Glasgow Concert Hall, St David's Hall Cardiff.

Recordings include: A Little Night Music, Merrily We Roll Along, Off The Wall, Body Works, Cabaret. Maria has just released her first solo album "Maria".

JAMES GOODE

Theatre includes: Three Sisters (Out of Joint tour), Macbeth (Committed Artists London & US tour); The White Devil, The Wind in the Willows (RNT); Blood Knot (Latchmere & US tour); King (Piccadilly); One Flew Over The Cuckoo's Nest (New Vic Co. tour); A Taste of Honey (Redgrave Farnham); Turaret (Gate); Crowned With Fame, Mass (RSC); American Clock (York).

Television includes: South of the Border, Watch, Return of Shelley.

BERNARD GALLAGHER

For the Royal Court: The Libertine, The Man of Mode (and Out of Joint), Carnival War A-Go-Hot, The Dragon, Crete and Sgt. Pepper.

Other theatre includes: Three Sisters (Out of Joint tour), School For Wives (Almeida); Getting Married, Therese Raquin (Chichester); Hamlet (Bristol Old Vic); Gaslight (Greenwich); The Black Angel (King's Head); Educating Rita (Young Vic Tour); John Gabriel Borkman (Southampton); El Sid (Half Moon); Loot (Manchester Royal Exchange); Roll On 4 O'Clock (Lyric/Palace); The Country Wife (Leatherhead); Breezeblock Park (Whitehall); The National Health, Weapons Of Happiness, Jumpers (RNT); Tis Pity She's a Whore, Julius Caeser, The Alchemist (RSC).

Television includes: Harry, London's Burning, Brother Cadfael, Eastenders, The Bill, This Is David Lander, The Chief, First and Last, Count Down To War, Take The High Road, New Statesman, Prisoners of Childhood, Rockliffe's Babies, Casualty, Farrington Of The FO, Frankie And Johnnie, The Practice, Relative Strangers, Moonfleet, Rolling Home.

BARNABY KAY

For the Royal Court: The Libertine, The Man Of Mode (and Out of Joint).

Other theatre includes:Three Sisters (Out of Joint tour), The Winter's Tale, A Jovial Crew, The Changeling, The Winter's Tale, The Taming Of The Shrew Cowboys II(RSC);

Time And The Room (Gate).

Television includes: Ghostbusters of East Finchley, The Vet, Minder, Moonfleet.

LLOYD HUTCHINSON

For the Royal Court: Some Voices

Other theatre includes: Three Sisters (Out of Joint tour), The Merry Wives Of Windsor, (RNT); Playboy Of The Western World (Sheffield Crucible); School For Wives (Belfast Civic Arts Theatre and Dublin Festival); Travesties (RSC and Savoy); A Jovial Crew, The School Of The Night, Tamburlaine The Great Part I, Tamburlaine The Great Part II, The Art Of Success, Cowboys II (as director), The Last Days Of Don Juan, Troilus And Cressida, Edward II, Love's Labour's Lost, Curse Of The Starving Classes, The Pretenders, Events While Guarding The Bofurs Gun (RSC).

Television includes: The Bill, London's Burning, Making News, The Nightwatch, Scout.

JOHN A.LEONARD (sound designer)

John Leonard started work in theatre sound over twenty years ago and has not stopped yet. His most recent work includes Hamlet at the Belasco Theatre on Broadway, The Visit at Chichester Festival Theatre, Zenobia and Feast for the RSC.

JULIAN McGOWAN (designer)

For the Royal Court: The Steward of Christendom (Out of Joint tour),, Blood, American Bagpipes, Women Laughing (& Royal Exchange), The Treatment.

Other theatre designs include:Three Sisters (Out of Joint tour), Old Times (Wyndhams, Theatr Clwyd); Venice Preserved, The Possibilities, The LA Plays (Almeida); Don Juan (Manchester Royal Exchange); Making History (set only/RNT); Heart Throb (Bush); Princess Ivona (ATC); Surgeon of Honour (Cheek by Jowl); Prin (Lyric, Hammersmith & West End); Leonce and Lena (Sheffield Crucible); The Magic Mountain, The Tempest, Romeo and Juliet, Pericles, The Comedy of Errors (Oxford Stage Company); The Rivals, Man and Superman, Playboy of the Western World, Hedda Gabler (Glasgow Citizens); Imagine Drowning, Punchbag (Hampstead); Caesar & Cleopatra, Total Eclipse (Greenwich); Tess of the Durbervilles (West Yorkshire Playhouse); The Changeling (set only/ RSC); The Lodger (Royal Exchange & Hampstead); Abigails Party, A Dolls House (Theatr Clwyd); The Wives Excuse (RSC); Torquatto Tasso (Edinburgh Festival); Playing the Wife (Chichester Festival Theatre).

Opera includes: Cosi fan tutte (New Israeli Opera); Eugene Onegin (Scottish Opera); The Nightingale and the Rose, Siren Song (Almeida Opera Festival).

MADLENA NEDEVA

Theatre includes: Three Sisters (Out of Joint tour), Fellini (Belvoir St Theatre Sydney); Ghosts (Lyric Studio, Hammersmith), Oethe's Tasso (Lyric Hammersmith & tour); Marat/Sade (Leeds Playhouse); The Seagull, Cabaret (Lancaster Playhouse); Phaedra (New End, Hampstead); Love's Labour's Lost (Ludlow Festival); The Two Noble Kinsmen (Regents Park); Chamber Music (Edinburgh Festival); O'Dad Poor Dad, Sell Out (Young Vic).

Television includes: G.P (ABC Austrailia), The House of Elliot, The Gift, London Embassy, A Very Peculiar Practice, Freud, Quest For Love, The Robbers, The Ghost Sonata, Thank You Comrades, The Enigma Files, The Professionals, Disraeli, The House Of Bernarda Alba, Spaghetti Twostep.

Films include: The Pink Panther, The Lady Vanishes, Margaret of Anjou, Anima.

BRIAN PROTHEROE

For the Royal Court: The Duchess of Malfi, The London Cuckolds

Other theatre includes: Three Sisters (Out of Joint tour); Leave Him To Heaven (New London); Dispatches, Larkrise, Candleford, Long Voyage Home, The Iceman Cometh (RNT); Pump Boys and Dinettes (Piccadilly); Holy Days (Soho Poly); Our Own Kind (Bush); The Winter's Tale (Young Vic); Schippel The Plumber (Greenwich); Who's Afraid of Virginia Woolf, The Taming of the Shrew (West Yorkshire Playhouse & Open Air Theatre, Barbados); The Sisters Rosensweig (Old Vic); Lysistrata (Wyndhams); A Midsummer Night's Dream, Richard III (Regents Park).

Television includes: Reilly, Ace of Spies, To Have and to Hold, Henry IV Parts I,II & III, Richard III, Titus Andronicus, Gentlemen and Players, Shrinks, Natural Lies.

Brian is also a musician/composer.

GUY RETALLACK (assistant director)

Theatre includes: Three Sisters (Out of Joint tour); The Queen and I (tour); Ivan Vasilievich (BAC Studio 1); The Millionairess, The Master and Margarita (BAC Mainhouse); The New Apartment (Watermans Arts); The Basset Table (New End); Bligh (ETC).

As assistant director: The Liar, Marta (Old Vic); Grand Magic (Assembly Rooms); All My Sons, Romeo and Juliet (Oxford Stage Company).

CATHERINE RUSSELL

Theatre includes: Three Sisters (Out of Joint tour); Arms And The Man (Royal Exchange); The Idiot, The Tempest, Tartuffe, Blood Brothers, Arturo Ui (Swan Theatre, Worcester); Venus And Lucrece (Almeida); The Last Carnival (Birmingham Rep); Sailor Beware, The Ghost Train (Lyric Hammersmith).

Television includes: Airbase, Chelworth, The Bill, Sherlock Holmes, Poirot, The Vision Thing, Chandler & Co.

Films include: The Lake, Soft Top Hard Shoulder, Solitaire For Two, Clockwork Mice.

JEREMY SAMS (songs)

As composer theatre includes: Ghetto, The Wind in the Willows, Arcadia (RNT); The Merry Wives of Windsor, Measure for Measure, The Tempest, A Midsummer Night's Dream, The Merchant of Venice, Much Ado About Nothing, Hamlet, The Constant Couple, Hyde Park, Temptation, Speculators, Crimes in Hot Countries, Down Child, The Castle, Two Shakespearean Actors, Some American Abroad (and Lincoln Center New York) (RSC); The Sneeze, A Walk In The Woods, Talking Heads (West End).

Television includes: Nativity Blues, Welcome Home Comrades, Uncle Vanya, Old Times, Downtown Lagos. Persuasion, Tiger Bastable. Radio includes: A Glass of Blessings, Arcadia, The Wind in the Willows.

As translator: Leonce Und Lena (Sheffield Crucible); The Rehearsal (Almeida and West End); Beckett (West End); The Miser, Les Parents Terribles (and as *Indiscretions* on Broadway) (RNT). Opera translations include: Figaro's Wedding, The Magic Flute, Macbeth, The Force of Destiny, La Boheme (ENO); l'Etiole, The Thieving Magpie, Orpheus in the Underworld, Jonny Strikes Up, Le Roi Malgre Lui (Opera North); Zemire at Azot (Camden Opera); Cendrillon (Welsh Opera).

As director: Schippel the Plumber (Greenwich and Edinburgh Festival); The Card (Newbury Watermill); Entertaining Mr Sloane (Greenwich); The Wind in the Willows (Tokyo); Neville's Island (Nottingham Playhouse and West End); Forty Years On (West Yorkshire Playhouse); Maria Friedman by Special Arrangement (Donmar Warehouse and West End); Le Roi Malgre Lui (Opera North); Enjoy (Nottingham Playhouse); Wild Oats (RNT).

MAX STAFFORD-CLARK (director)

Following his Artistic Directorship of The Traverse Theatre, Edinburgh, he founded Joint Stock with William Gaskill. From 1979-1993 he was Artistic Director of the Royal Court Theatre. In 1993 he founded his touring company Out of Joint, and is currently an Associate Director of the Royal Court.

NIGEL TERRY

For the Royal Court: Blood Poetry, Prairie Du Chien, Victory, Operation Bad Apple, Light Shining In Buckinghamshire, Traps, The Fool, Big Wolf.

Other theatre includes: Three Sisters (Out of Joint tour); seasons at RSC; Royal National Theatre; Manchester '69; and Sheffield Crucible. Television includes: The Mushroom Picker, The Orchid House, Rules of Engagement, Jackanory, The Vet, Pie in the Sky, Resort to Murder.

Films include: Excalibur, Lion in Winter; and for Derek Jarman, *Caravaggio, Edward II, Last of England, War Requiem, Blue*.

JOHANNA TOWN (lighting designer)

For the Royal Court: Pale Horse, The Steward of Christendom (Out of Joint), Ashes and Sand, The Editing Process, Peaches, Babies, The Kitchen, Search and Destroy, Women Laughing, Faith Healer.

Other theatre lighting designs include: Three Sisters, Road (Out of Joint tour); Disappeared (Leicester Haymarket & tour); The Lodger (Royal Exchange & Hampstead); Richard II, Street Captives (Royal Exchange); Stiff Stuff (Library Theatre, Manchester); Soldiers (CO Producers); Trafford Tanzi (London Bubble); Salvation, The Snow Orchid (London Gay Theatre); The Set-Up, Crackwalker (Gate Theatre); Josephine (BAC and tour); Celestina (ATC); Beautiful Thing (Bush, Donmar, Duke of Yorks); over 20 designs for Liverpool Playhouse including Macbeth, The Beaux Stratagem, Madame Mao.

Opera includes: The Marriage of Figaro, Eugene Onegin, The Abduction from the Seraglio, The Merry Widow (Opera 80); The Human Voice, Perfect Swine (MTM); The Poison Chalice, The Magic Flute, La Traviata (MTL at the Donmar and in Hamburg); Otello (Opera du Nice). Currently Chief Electrician at the Royal Court.

JEROME WILLIS

For the Royal Court: Killers

Other theatre includes: Three Sisters (Out of Joint tour), The Life of Galileo (Almeida); The Bacchae, Ghost Sonata (Queen Elizabeth Hall); Himself, A Piece of My Mind, The Ambassador, Roll on Friday (Nuffield Southampton & tour); In Broad Daylight (Nuffield Southampton & Tricycle); The Double Dealer (Tour); Totally Foxed (Queens Theatre Hornchurch); The Late Christopher Bean, Back to Methuselah (Cambridge Theatre Co.tour); Pork Pies (Stratford East); Medea-Euripedes (Lyric Hammersmith); Pygmalion (Oxford Playhouse & tour); Educating Rita (Derby Playhouse), Antony and Cleopatra (Ludlow Festival); Rules of the Game (West End & tour); No Man's Land (Haymarket Leicester).

Television includes: Mind to Murder, Space Precinct, Blue Heaven, Goodnight Sweetheart, True Crimes, Unnatural Causes, The Harry Enfield Show, Stay Lucky, Underbelly, Incident at Victoria Falls, Sherlock Holmes and the Leading Lady, Black and Blue, Fabulous Singlettes, The New Statesman, Chain, Wish Me Luck, 68 Highmere Park, The Gentlemen's Club, Running Wild, Yes Prime Minister, Oedipus at Colonnus, To Have and To Hold, Bergerac, Tender is the Night, Pickwick Papers, Oscar, By the Sword Divided, The Tales of Beatrix Potter Films include: Tales of Mystery and Imagination, Business Affairs, Orlando, Dear Sarah, Death of a Son, Tyndale, Anastasia, Space Vampires.

The Royal Court Theatre and Out of Joint would like to thank the following for their generosity and help with this production: Bodum UK; Caroline Boocock; Boots Company Plc; City Clocks Ltd; Dolland and Aitchsion; Imperial Tobacco Ltd; Peter Jones (Sloane Square) 0171 730 3434; The London Herb and Spice Company; Cutlery supplied by Mapin and Webb; Normand City of London (Mercedes-Benz); Paperchase; Parker Pens Ltd; Glassware supplied by Stuart Crystal; Timex Watches; Truefit and Hill - Gentlemen's Grooming 0171 493 2961; United Distillers UK; Champagne by Veuve Clicquot Ponsardin; West 9 Coffee Ltd 01923 210710; Wardrobe care by Persil and Comfort supplied by Lever Brothers Ltd; watches by The Timex Corporation; refrigerators by Electrolux and Philips Major Appliances Ltd; kettles for rehearsals by Morphy Richards; video for casting purposes by Hitachi; hair by Rick Strickland; furniture by Knoll International; freezer for backstage use supplied by Zanussi Ltd; 'Now thats a good idea'; Closed circuit TV cameras and monitors by Mitsubishi UK Ltd; natural spring water from Wye Spring Water, 149 Sloane Street, London SW1, tel. 0171 730 6977; overhead projector from WH Smith; Krups UK Ltd, Sanyo U.K for the backstage microwave; Sodastream.

How the Royal Court is brought to you

The English Stage Company at the Royal Court Theatre is supported financially by a wide range of public bodies and private companies, as well as its own trading activities. The theatre receives its principal funding from the **Arts Council of England**, which has supported the Royal Court since 1956. The **Royal Borough of Kensington & Chelsea** gives an annual grant to the Royal Court Young Peoples Theatre and provides some of its staff. The **London Boroughs Grants Committee** contributes to the cost of productions in the Theatre Upstairs.

Other parts of the Royal Court's activities are made possible by business sponsorships. Several of these sponsors have made a long-term commitment.
1995 has seen the fifth Barclays New Stages Festival of Independent Theatre, which has been supported throughout by **Barclays Bank**. **British Gas North Thames** supported three years of the Royal Court's Education Programme. The latest sponsorship by **WH Smith** helped to make the launch of the Friends of the Royal Court scheme so successful.

1993 saw the start of our association with the **Audrey Skirball-Kenis Theatre**, of Los Angeles. The Skirball Foundation is funding a Playwrights Programme at the Royal Court. Exchange visits for writers between Britain and the USA complement the greatly increased programme of readings and workshops which have fortified the Royal Court's capability to develop new plays.

In 1988 the Royal Court launched the **Olivier Building Appeal** to raise funds to restore, repair and improve the theatre building. So far nearly £750,000 has been raised. The theatre has new bars and front of house areas, new roofs, air conditioning and central heating boilers, a rehearsal room and a completely restored and cleaned facade. This would not have been possible without a large number of generous supporters and significant contributions from the **Theatres Restoration Fund**, the **Rayne Foundation**, the **Foundation for Sport and the Arts** and the **Arts Councils Incentive Funding Scheme**.

The Royal Court earns the rest of the money it needs to operate from the Box Office, from other trading and from the transfers of plays such as **Death and the Maiden**, **Six Degrees of Separation**, **Oleanna** and **My Night With Reg** to the West End. But without public subsidy it would close immediately and its unique place in British Theatre would be lost. If you care about the future of arts in this country, please write to your MP and say so.

Join the Royal Court's
Mailing List

ROYAL COURT THEATRE

For just £5
a year you will receive advance information
*on **ALL** productions at the Royal Court*
***PLUS** exclusive special offers*

For further information the
Royal Court Box Office on **0171 730 5174**

Invest in the future

share more fully in the life of the Royal Court Theatre... become a Patron or Benefactor.

Join our supporters, and share in the opportunity to ensure the continuation of one of the world's most famous theatres, whilst enjoying a number of exclusive benefits which will enhance your theatregoing throughout the year.

For more information please call the Royal Court Box Office on 0171 730 1745.

PATRONS
Greg Dyke
Spencer & Calla Fleischer
Richard Pulford
Sir George Russell
Richard Wilson
Irene Worth

CORPORATE PATRONS
Advanpress
Berisford PLC
Bunzl PLC
Citigate Communications
Criterion Productions PLC
Dibb Lupton Broomhead
Sue Gregory for The
Draycott Hotel
Homevale Ltd
Lex Service PLC
Laporte PLC
The Mirror Group PLC
New Penny Productions Ltd
News Corporation Ltd
Noel Gay Artists/Hamilton
Asper Management
Angela Pope & The Peter
Cole Foundation
The Simkins Partnership
Simons Muirhead and
Burton
Skylight Productions-
Munich & New York
Touche Ross & Co.

ASSOCIATES
Robyn Durie
Nicholas A Fraser
Henny Gestetner OBE
Peter Jones
Patricia Marmont
Barbara Minto
John Mortimer
Greville Poke
Geoffrey Strachan

BENEFACTORS
David H. Adams
Derek Brierley
Julia Brodie
Julian Brookstone
Carole & Neville Conrad
Conway van Gelder
David Coppard & Co
Curtis Brown Ltd
Allan Davis
Peter A Deal
Robert Dufton
Anthony M Fry
Murray Gordon
Rocky Gottlieb
Stephen Gottlieb
Angela Heylin
Andre Hoffman
Jane How
Institute of Practitioners in
Advertising
Sahra Lese
Lady Lever
Merrill Lynch
Pat Morton

Michael Orr
Carol Rayman
Angharad Rees
B. J & Rosemary Reynolds
John Sandoe (Books) Ltd
Nicholas Selmes
Lord Sheppard
John Thorpe
Tomkins plc
Eric Walters
Sue Weaver, The Sloane
Club
William Morris Agency

The Break of Day

for D.

Act One

The garden of a small country house in the middle of summer. Lawn, some flowers. Nothing grand, but beautiful and peaceful. It is early morning. **Tess Warner** *is sitting with a huge pile of newspapers, which she is scanning very fast. She cuts out one small item.* **Nina Sehn** *comes out in a dressing gown. The women kiss on the cheeks.*

Nina You're working.

Tess I wanted to get this done before breakfast.

Nina Can I help?

Tess Scan. Anything to do with women. Something individual. It'll be buried in the back pages.

Nina looks.

Nina Here: 'Fertility begins at forty.' It's about gardening.

Tess Here's one: 'Many of the motorway protesters who live for months in trees are women.' 'Women who live in trees', that's a good title. Or, as my old paper would put it: 'The passions of a tree girlie.'

Nina I could do that –

Tess Nina, they don't have bathtubs up there.

Nina More than eighty per cent of England is within hearing distance of a busy road. It drives me mad.

Tess Does it disturb the music in your head?

Nina It disturbs the silence in my head.

3

Tess You could write a song about it.

Nina Joni Mitchell did it twenty years ago: 'They've paved paradise and put up a parking lot.' You can't write that song now.

Tess When we first met you were writing those types of songs. You'd formed your band.

Nina That's right … you came to interview us.

Tess I remember every moment of that night, don't you?

Nina I never think about the past.

Tess I felt so powerful. There you were, an all-female band, and I was the only woman reporter on a rock magazine. Women were exploding everywhere, with their anger, hunger, confidence, all those possibilities. We talked all night, you must remember.

Nina I must have met Hugh then. He was sent by his record company.

Tess That was because they realized women even had the power to sell albums. It was almost exactly twenty years ago – a week after my twentieth birthday.

Nina Your birthday, why didn't you say?

Tess I'm celebrating it this weekend.

Nina Now I understand. That's why April is coming.

Tess I can't believe she sang with you.

Nina Her voice was wonderful, but she only wanted the money to get her through university.

Tess Our formidable professor of classics.

Nina I hope she doesn't terrify everyone.

Tess I'll keep her under control. We'll have a great weekend. We'll send the men off to play tennis and we'll com-memorate.

Nina I don't like to remember.

Tess That's because you're so secretive. I remember those consciousness raising sessions, we'd all be describing our orgasms or lack of them in great detail and you'd say you had to protect the identity of your lover.

Nina Hugh was married at the time.

Tess As if orgasms have anything to do with the identity of the male. You were better once you were with Robert. Actually, I have a confession to make … It was the way you described Robert that made me decide I wanted him.

Nina I see.

Tess I felt I had a right to what I wanted. It goes with the empowerment I felt all my life. Born into this heroic empire – that's what they taught us – educated, national-healthed. Then the sixties when all you had to do was be very young. Being a woman in the seventies, then being in London and clever in the eighties, making money despite myself, buying this house. And now –

Nina Now?

Tess That's why you're here.

Nina I'm the last person who should be here.

Tess You succeeded where you wanted to – like me.

Nina I'm not doing anything, I'm a kind of traitor.

Tess Hugh says you've been working on new songs.

Nina What?

Tess I want to hear them. April will analyse our lives for us and then, then – I'll feel empowered again. We all will.

5

Nina Tess: I don't have any new songs.

Hugh *comes in.*

Tess Aren't you planning another album?

Nina (*to Hugh*) Is that what you're saying?

Hugh What a perfect morning. Clear, green, English. I still love this country – although it's not as green as it used to be: look at your grass.

Tess You need someone to play tennis. Where's Robert? He's just been offered two jobs at once, after a year not working.

Nina (*to Hugh*) Why are you saying I'm working on a new album?

Hugh Isn't that good for Robert?

Tess One of them is a Chekhov in a tiny company for no money, the other is a television. Poor Robert. It's going to be a weekend of agonized indecision, he's probably still in bed with the duvet over his head, I'll go and get him for you.

Hugh You're the perfect hostess.

Tess I've looked forward to this weekend – I want to celebrate, remake old friendships. When Jamie comes you can have a powerful foursome.

Tess leaves.

Nina Why are you saying I'm working on a new album?

Hugh Because you are. You may not know it.

Nina There's nothing in my head.

Hugh It's not there yet.

Nina You need the successful album.

Hugh Yes, but so do you. I have other artists.

Nina So why are you pushing me?

Hugh I'm trying to help you, I think you'll be happier if you get some songs out –

Nina You seem to think I'm suppressing them. I tell you, they're not there.

Hugh Does that make you happy?

Nina No.

Hugh Then make an effort!

Nina You know it's not that simple. Anyway, I have other things on my mind.

Hugh I know, Nina, but you also have your work, it's in your control. That's what you do best.

Nina How can I know? I haven't tried anything else. I should get dressed. (*She doesn't move.*)

Hugh I love you. I want you to be happy. What's wrong with a happy marriage? Is it oppressive or something?

Nina Sometimes I feel I have to redeem you because you made your first wife so unhappy.

Hugh All I want is to enjoy this weekend, play tennis, get you to write one song.

Nina Tess is raking up the past – how we stood in front of life with all those possibilities – not because we were young but because it was that moment. I don't feel powerful at all, is that because of this moment? But since you only see with the eyes given to you by the moment you live in, how can you fight it? Who'll give you the map showing the passage out?

Hugh There you are. Work it out.

7

Nina I can't, that's the point. I'll get dressed.

Hugh Will you wake Nick up?

Nina He's your son.

Hugh Nina –

Nina All right. I'll knock on his door. If he growls at me?

Hugh Growl back.

Nina goes off. Hugh *is alone.* **Paul**, *the gardener, comes on.*

Paul The question of happiness. Men never ask themselves if they are happy, they just have heart attacks. I'm Paul, I do Tess's garden. I remember your wife's first album. Sensational.

Hugh Don't tell her that.

Paul I have a girlfriend now, she says she'll be happy if I marry her. I think to myself, at least this is an unhappiness we both understand. I want to keep it that way. If it doesn't rain soon, this lawn is going to die, all the lawns of England will die, all the gardens will wither. We'll have to do what they do in California and create desert gardens, but California is yellow anyway, whereas England is deep green. That would make me unhappy, if England became yellow. I've never understood how people can leave England for Greece and Spain.

He goes off. **April** *comes on.*

Hugh April. You look well.

April I'm exhausted.

Hugh Is it Sappho?

April Sweet of you to remember. Jamie always asks which Greek lady I'm writing about. No, it's the government. I used to teach. You know, talk to students, share learning. Now I fill in forms. I won't bore you with it.

Hugh It interests me.

April You Americans are always so courteous. This is a country where you don't need to act any more, you only need to describe actions on paper. My students don't ask me questions, they assess me. Was this teacher (a) very good, (b) mediocre, (c) unspeakable? What kind of dialogue is that? The easier I make things for them, that is, the less I teach them, the more they like me. Stop me. I've already ruined the morning. I wanted to have a romantic drive down with Jamie, I went on and on, he's now escaped to his mobile. How is Nina?

Hugh Inactive. Give her some lines of Sappho.

    Natasha *comes on and brings them coffee.*

April They're only fragments. Fragments every generation fills.

Hugh That's what songs are. Fragments of a generation. Tell me more about Sappho.

    Natasha leaves.

April There's your American politeness again. Who's that?

Hugh I'm Jewish, April, I like to know everything that's going on. I like to know about my musicians' lives. I'm not creative, I facilitate, mix, edit, but I'm always fascinated by what my artists pick up from the world. Why are young people returning to lyricism in music, why Sappho for you?

    Natasha comes back on with croissants.

April A mystery. A woman about whom we know nothing, revered as the best among the best Greek poets.

Thank you.

Natasha bows and goes.

Who is she?

Hugh One of Tess's servants it seems. Please talk to Nina about Sappho. Inspire her.

April To what?

Hugh Her third album. She has to do it.

April Why?

Hugh That's what she is.

April Are you sure?

Hugh I know these artists. They all get mesmerized by this idea of silence, because they're angry or they want to punish themselves. It's no good. You've seen Nina in front of an audience, you know it's the closest she comes to happiness.

April I'd like to find someone who loved me that much.

Hugh It's a burden I place on her.

April I could take it. Will you help me in exchange?

Hugh It's a deal.

April Talk to Jamie. It's been a year. He can't commit himself to living with me. He's even nervous about spending a night together in his sister's house. You can talk sense to him. There must be something that can be unlocked. We have a great time together then suddenly – tell me, am I frightening?

Hugh Not to me.

April Convince him.

Jamie *comes on, distraught.*

Jamie How do you start a revolution?

Hugh Hi, Jamie.

Jamie Apparently there's an article in the papers. (*He tears through the papers.*) It must have been something like this that led to the peasants' revolt, the Russian revolution. One day, you say, I've had enough, how dare you do this, to me, to us.

April What's happened?

Jamie We could organize a sit-in, I'll shoot if I have to.

April Jamie, I left you five minutes ago with your mobile checking up on a little girl whose hand you'd saved.

Jamie is still tearing through the papers.

Jamie Here it is. I was good in chemistry.

Tess comes on with Nina. They kiss April. Jamie ignores them.

I know how to make a bomb.

Tess What's going on?

April We're trying to find out.

Hugh Jamie seems to want to join the Baader-Meinhof.

Tess Have you told him he's thirty years too late? What's wrong?

Jamie We've got to stop it. Tess, you've stopped things in your time. Greenham Common, all that.

Tess You can't become political overnight.

Jamie I just have.

Tess If I said I'd become a surgeon overnight, I wouldn't be allowed near a hospital. Stay away. You'll look silly. Tell us what's upset you and then let's forget about it.

Jamie Forget about it? They want to close down the whole hospital. It's in here! My hospital, the oldest, the best. I've worked all my life to become a consultant in a big NHS hospital. There's been nowhere better to be. Yesterday I saved a girl's hand. It took twelve hours. Finger by finger, vein by vein, one millimetre at a time. You get one finger sewn back in three hours and you ask yourself, why are there so many damn fingers to a hand. But I did it. Not just me. My team. Together for ten years. I need to make five hundred different requests during such an operation. My theatre sister knows what I want before I ask. I hold out my hand, the instrument is there. The child will be able to move all her fingers. They want to close us down. I don't understand. It can't be the country that wants this: when I was only a junior doctor in Wales, they dressed up to see me, they called me Sir.

April They tried to close the classics department at my university. We fought.

Jamie Did you win?

April We compromised. We no longer teach Greek and Latin. It's classics in translation, without the bone, the beauty of the original language. And the classes trebled. We thought we'd won, but I suppose really we lost. Now they want us to make the degrees easier. We take weak students, we give them a good degree, they haven't learned anything but the university looks good.

Jamie I won't accept that.

April Dictatorships use force. Democracies convince you you are wrong.

Nina Or make you feel there's no value in speaking.

Robert *comes on with an old-fashioned racket in its press.*

Robert I'm a terrible host, I'm sorry. I was reading all night. Natasha's bringing more coffee and croissants for the women and I understand the men are playing tennis.

Jamie I'm not playing.

Tess You have to play.

Robert We have to do what Tess wants, we're celebrating her birthday.

Jamie It was last week.

Tess If you remembered, why didn't you send me a card?

Jamie I'm your brother, why should I send you a card?

April I remembered, I brought you a fabulous new translation of Marcus Aurelius, you know, the Stoic, my students love it.

Robert We're celebrating this weekend. We're playing tennis.

Tess I thought you'd all enjoy a good men's game. It's what you like doing together, isn't it, sport?

Robert I spent the whole night reading Chekhov's stories. The men never play sports, they talk. They talk endlessly. I envy civilizations where talking itself is a sport. I'd like to come to you now and ask you all to help me make a decision. I can play Vershinin or I can play in a television series about hospitals. It's badly written and the subject's been done many times before. But it's money. I feel embarrassed even saying this, the decision must seem unimportant. Being an actor is unimportant.

Tess Robert, this isn't talk, it's a melancholic soliloquy.

Robert I'm sorry.

Jamie I thought people watched things like *Dynasty* to

escape. Now it seems the summit of people's fantasies in England is to be treated in an NHS hospital by a consultant like me.

Robert I shouldn't do it.

Tess He didn't say that.

Nina You shouldn't do it.

Robert I haven't worked for a year. It's well paid. I can't let Tess have all the responsibility – although – have you told them?

Tess No …

Robert Why not?

Tess It's not definite.

Nina What?

Robert It looks like Tess is going to be made the Editor of her magazine.

Nina You mean you're going to run it, that's wonderful!

April You can make some changes.

Tess Why?

April I was reading it last night and there are aspects I find unacceptable.

Robert I am so proud of Tess. Her own magazine.

April Yes, but she has to make it a worthwhile magazine.

Nina April, we can't all read the *TLS*.

Hugh That's a wonderful racket, Robert.

Robert I got it from a series. That was a good series, I had a small part but I was pleased to be in it.

Tess You don't have to do it.

Robert How can I tour for nine months for no money with a tiny theatre company no one will watch? And yet, last night, I opened the door on a whole world. And those three sisters suspended in an odd paralysis at the end of their century, with a cataclysm already in formation. There's something familiar about that paralysis, feeling outside history, I wanted to explore it – well – (*Pause.*) Even learn Russian. I didn't go to university like Tess, sometimes I get to learn on the job. I could if I did the part – but it's not responsible. Being an actor isn't responsible. It might be if it were valued. I keep reading articles on why no one wants to go to the theatre. I'm convinced.

April You see: democracy. You'll soon be convinced no one needs medicine: if people looked after themselves better, they wouldn't get sick in the first place.

Hugh I think you're forgetting you can also change things in a democracy.

Nina Not if you can't see them clearly. I walk out in the streets. I see a blur of misery, but I don't know where to focus. Isn't that what April is saying? In this country, you're not encouraged to look.

Tess You mean look at the negative –

Robert Chekhov makes you look, but what's the point if nobody goes to look at him. Even Tess doesn't go to the theatre, except to mega-openings.

Tess I have to be seen. I don't always like it.

Robert I'm not complaining. Certainly one isn't seen on the opening night of a small touring company in Worthing. Let's play tennis.

Jamie Chekhov was a doctor, wasn't he? Why did he give

it up?

Robert He didn't. That's what's so extraordinary. He – never mind.

Nina You should do what you want.

Tess That's what I say.

Robert But you don't mean it.

Nina Hugh says that to me, he says he'll produce any song I write, but he really wants me to sing something that will be a hit single.

Hugh That's a complete lie: I've always let you follow your caprices –

Nina Caprice.

Hugh Even you admit that feminist collective of yours was a caprice.

April You're not talking about our band!

Hugh No, that was fresh, it wasn't even that feminist.

April We disguised it.

Hugh After Nina's first album she decided to rebel and got mixed up with these women who spent all their time discussing whether they could allow a male producer and a capitalistic record company to interfere. It was a complete disaster, of course –

Nina Nobody promoted it.

Hugh Every interview was vetoed if it was a male interviewer. We couldn't find a cover, nobody would dress as anything. We said to you, be really masculine if you want, be really feminine, just be something – men in the music business usually make themselves really feminine and they look great. OK, they don't have thousands of years of

16

exploitation behind them, but we had a record to sell. Then there was your rustic phase, playing to yourself in the back of remote pubs, bringing poetry to rural areas or whatever you were doing –

Nina That was a great time. I took up riding.

Hugh But the music was bad.

Nina Does anybody care?

Hugh I did and so did your record company. Then total silence from you.

Nina You said yourself no one was interested in songs any more, kids were mixing the sounds themselves –

Hugh That's changed. The record company wants a third album from you, it's in your contract, what can I do to make her do it, what?

April You can't push her.

Tess I'd do an interview with you.

Nina I hate publicity.

Tess That's not integrity, Nina, that's suicide.

Nina I have a right to silence.

Hugh No, you don't!

Nina And then, England … it sort of makes you silent.

Hugh It's the government's fault now, is it?

Nina You treat me like a perverse child who's refusing to cooperate. You have no idea what it's like, day after day, trawling for the phrase, the feeling, that'll catch the song. But when I get a glimpse, I think, no, it's not important.

April That's the discomfort of democracy. Everyone can speak, so all words have equal value, or none at all.

Tess I've loved every song you've written.

April So have I. Well, most.

Nina I was reading about Eastern Europe the other day, and the writer says culture is what allows society to understand itself. What struck me most was his confidence in using that word. I used to love that title: singer-songwriter. It feels meaningless. Using words, it's called chatter. Music, it's called sounds.

Robert I can understand that sense of worthlessness. I used to think I could change the world.

April I lecture to seventy students at a time, I'm already telling these kids they're worthless, there are too many of them for me even to remember their names. At Oxbridge, they would have one so-called eminent tutor, looking after them, one to one, valued –

Jamie I have this young patient who was born with a terrible face tumour. I've done seventeen operations on her. The last one would have restored her ear, but apparently some ear quota had been filled. I watched this withdrawn miserable child turn into an increasingly confident girl, but finally some manager decided her future happiness was too expensive.

Hugh Americans have always overcome their feelings of worthlessness by being in love with the future. Once you lose that, the rot really sets in.

Robert Chekhov seems to love the future, I'm not sure I do.

Jamie Does anyone in this country even believe in the future any more?

April I still do. I know that at least one of my nameless students will come into contact with an ancient, wise and passionate mind and ignite.

Tess It's the present that counts. I commission articles where women or children have triumphed against all odds. Now.

Nina To sing, you have to believe someone will be there to listen to you, not only now – in the future.

Robert If there is a future, by that I mean a future with language – I should speak the lines of Chekhov. If there isn't – it doesn't matter what I do.

Pause.

Tess It's not even lunchtime and we're all depressed sitting talking around a cafetière.

Robert The Russians sat around their samovar, talking –

Tess Look what happened to them.

Robert Time to play tennis.

Nick *comes on.*

There's our fourth.

Tess Did you sleep well?

Hugh What do you think about England, Nick?

Nick Not much, I mean, I don't think about it. Dad, listen …

Hugh Aren't students concerned?

Nick They're worried about money, Dad …

Tess What do they think about the world?

Nick Yeah. Dad, listen, what's happened is, look, Marisa's here.

Hugh Marisa?

Nick Remember? I told you, my girlfriend.

Hugh The beautiful blonde one?

Nick No, that was ages ago. You haven't met her. She's – well, she hasn't wanted – but look, she's here.

Nina You didn't invite her!

Nick No, I don't know how she found me, I mean, anyway, she's waiting, at the station, she's been travelling all night, she's just called –

Nina Aren't you going back to college on Monday?

Nick It's – she says it's important, she's waiting, Dad …

Hugh All right, we'll go and get her, is she as nice as the last one?

Nick No, I mean, she's different, she's not like – I mean, she doesn't come from a family like this, you know, arty-farty, she's more – she's political too.

Nina We like that.

Nick Not like you, I mean, Nina, you and Dad, you'd drive two cars to an anti-traffic demo. Marisa doesn't even wear leather –

Tess We're having roast lamb for lunch.

Nick Maybe there's a vegetarian caff, we can stop on the way –

Tess This is the countryside, Nick, there's one pub, it'll be serving roast beef. She can have lots of birthday cake.

Nick She, you see, she doesn't believe in birthdays –

Tess I thought a birthday only oppressed the one who was having it.

Nick It's not that – well, she'll tell you herself, she's very

20

together about it – I don't believe in birthdays either. Dad, you always forget mine.

Nina He forgets his own, Nick, he doesn't want to get old.

Nick Dad ... Please –

Hugh and Nick go out.

Tess I'll see what I have in the kitchen. Robert, if you find Paul you could ask him if we have any vegetables, or herbs, or flowers she can eat –

Nina I'll come with you, I'm good on herbs.

Tess, Robert and Nina leave. April and Jamie are left alone. Pause.

Jamie I should go and ring some colleagues.

April If you want to mount a campaign for your hospital I can help you. There's a way of going about these things, using the press, everyone you know who knows some-body, getting to the prime minister for five minutes, it's quite disgusting in some ways, but you can win. (*Pause.*) What's wrong? You're giving me that look again.

Jamie What?

April Don't come close. Keep off, predator. I can't accept it any more. Why do you always make me feel I'm invad-ing your territory?

Jamie This is such a shock for me.

April And I want to help you.

Jamie I know, but –

April Accepting my help would be some kind of commit-ment and you can't – I'm tired of being at the edge of your life. You should decide – now.

Jamie This isn't the right place, the right time –

April It is. Tess and Nina have men in their lives, what I call daytime men, they're there, in broad daylight, I have a twilight man –

Jamie Thanks.

April There for the evening, dinner, the first half of the night –

Jamie I operate in the mornings.

April You know what I'm saying –

Jamie All Tess, Robert, Hugh and Nina do is argue and complain about each other in public –

April I'll even accept that, it's part of the daytime man. I don't have to have it now, but I have to know it's going to happen.

Jamie I don't even know what's going to happen to my hospital.

April You can't wait for a new government to make an emotional commitment.

Jamie April, I have to ring my colleagues –

April I want an answer.

Jamie If you want an answer right now –

April I can wait until tonight, even tomorrow if we spend the night here. This is so humiliating …

Jamie I'm sorry …

> *He leaves. April is alone. She slaps herself. Natasha comes on. She sits next to April and touches her hand.*

April I'm sorry?

Natasha Sappho.

April Are you Greek? Are you from Lesbos?

Natasha Lesbos. Sappho.

She lunges at April and kisses her.

April What are you doing!

Natasha Sappho.

Tess comes on.

Tess Natasha! What's going on?

April I think we're having a cultural misunderstanding.

Natasha Sappho, you say: Sappho.

April That's the point of my book. She wasn't gay, at least not in the way we understand the word, it's a historical misunderstanding –

Tess I'll have to fire her, she's mad.

April Baffled, lonely, in a foreign country. In America once, I was very flattered by the attentions of a male student, until I realized he wanted me to pay him. That was supposedly the same language.

Tess She knocked on the door looking for work, I assumed she was from Bosnia. She's probably from Cardiff.

April You can't be gay and a war victim?

Tess Where are you from?

Natasha Kitchen. I go –

She goes. Robert and Nina come in.

Robert Paul gave us some dandelions, some nasturtiums, every herb in *Hamlet* and he said he'd ask our neighbour

Mr Hardacre for tomatoes. He's doing wonderful things in the garden, how much do we pay him?

Tess You mean how much do I pay him –

Robert Fine. I'll take the telly.

Tess I didn't – I'm sorry, April's almost been raped by a Bosnian. I don't know what to do about lunch – I wanted this to be such a good day.

April I'll go and apologize to the poor woman, she should really apologize to me. Have you noticed we're the most arrogant nation on earth but we always apologize? But no, I should apologize –

Tess Why?

April Because we don't know where she's from, and her life has ceased to interest us, although we cry for her on television, because our imagination has been depleted by this terrible century – because words like compassion and humanity have cracked in the last fifteen years and we've let it happen –

Tess It's Jamie, isn't it? Do you want me to talk to him?

April What can you say?

Tess I'll tell him how odd and wonderful you are.

April He knows that, it's not the problem.

Tess and April leave.

Robert In *Three Sisters* the characters contemplate the end of their century with that same sense of waste, of being outside history, but Vershinin intoxicates himself with a vision of a better future. I don't believe Chekhov intends to mock that. He kept building schools: humanity could become better.

Nina My grandmother started life like one of those sisters, but then she found herself in St Petersburg during the famine. She often told me how she went in search of bread to bring back to her son, my father, but ate it all on the way back. I don't think she was a very good mother. My father said she kept him in short trousers so she would seem younger and remarry and get out. A lot of those Russians went around missing their estates, but I think she enjoyed it, migration, husbands, lovers, history. Even when she was old she kept moving house. I have her restlessness and I envy her experience of history.

Robert Ninotchka, you never told me about her. You were always so secretive.

Nina You weren't playing Vershinin.

Robert I'm not playing him now. How can I? Tess and I want children, did she tell you? Aren't you still her best friend?

Nina Friendship is like marriage, there are Siberian wastes you don't cross.

Robert She'd sort of forgotten about it in the heady eighties, I reminded her we ought to start. I think she thought it would be like everything else and she would have two perfect children then and there. She went to the women's magazine to have more time – you can't really have a child if you're on a daily. That was three years ago. We don't talk about it. I study the calendar secretly. It's beginning to feel like Lorca's *Yerma*. All last year I was thinking how nice it would be to take my children to the park, but I wasn't working. If there's going to be a child, I ought to do the telly, otherwise … I would love to do Vershinin … Did they ever find out what was wrong? I'm sorry, is it painful for you?

Nina I keep hoping. And there are other ways …

Robert Tell me …

Nina Is that why you left me?

Robert I left you because you did nothing to keep me.

Nina There were so many men, so many possibilities. Some of my friends solved the problem by sampling a lot of men at once, I could only do it serially. You were better than most because you were an actor so you paraded a lot of different men in my life, but then I never had you …

Robert I never had myself … In Chekhov there's one moment when two people might come together and find happiness, but one hesitates, or makes a wrong move, and those people's chance is over, for ever …

Nina We felt we had an infinite number of chances …

Robert Will you stay faithful to Hugh?

Nina Yes. It's less tiring mentally. But whenever I think I'm happy, I begin to feel this gnawing in my stomach and that worm eating out the black hole that women can never fill. I tried to write a song about it once, this void inside us, insatiable, unfillable. You don't have it.

Robert We work, we think about the future.

Nina We work. It's still there. It's worse because we can no longer say it's because we have nothing to do.

Robert Children …

Nina … not to fill the void.

Robert But to fill the future …

Nina I compose lullabies in my head. I can't tell Hugh.

Robert Nina, I miss you.

Nina Don't.

They embrace. Tess comes on.

We were remembering.

Tess I've been remembering all weekend. Is this my retribution?

Nina I never really forgave you.

Tess What's feminism for if we still hate each other?

Nina It's a peace treaty, not a love feast.

Nina and Tess go off.

Robert 'How can I put it? It seems to me that everything in the world must gradually change – two hundred years hence, three hundred years … eventually a new and happy life will dawn.'

Robert shakes his head. **Marisa** *rushes through.*

Marisa I'm going to be sick.

She comes back and looks at Robert and screams.

You're that rapist. On the television.

Robert I played a rapist. I'm an actor.

Marisa Yeah. And you're that father.

Robert No …

Marisa In that film, the one who sleeps with this girl but doesn't know she's his daughter, that could have been me, I mean, I don't know who my father is.

Robert I'm sure it's not me.

Marisa Where were you in October 1973?

Robert I can't remember, probably on tour in the north of England.

Marisa There you are. My mother was in the north of England. She can't remember. She was drunk. I'd know if I was sleeping with my father. How come she didn't know?

Robert I don't know, I didn't ask her.

Marisa You were sleeping with her!

Robert Only in the film. We did what the director told us.

Marisa It's terrible not to know who your father is, how could he have done that, my dad? I think men should take responsibility, don't you?

Robert Yes.

Marisa I'm going to be sick again. No. It's gone.

Robert I think you want to speak to Nick about this.

Marisa How can you know what I want?

Robert It's my job as an actor, finding out what someone wants. I'll call him.

Marisa I wanted to tell them in the car but his dad kept talking about raves. Weird. I guess he wanted to be friendly, but I like opera. My favourite video is *Bluebeard's Castle*, by Bartok, do you know it? I could have been a musician. In my last foster home, they had a piano, but it was too late. I suppose Nick told you I was in care. I'm not ashamed of it, it wasn't my fault, people look at you as if it was. I was lucky, I wasn't abused, but two of the families were struck off. The one with the piano, they loved me, but I was already sixteen, they couldn't keep me.

Nick comes on.

Nick Lunch is almost ready, Nina's made a nasturtium

28

salad, it looks great, come and meet everybody.

Robert Marisa has something to say to you. I'll send Tess out as well. (*to Marisa*) I think it's good news. (*He goes.*)

Nick What?

Marisa He's nice for a duvvie –

Nick A what?

Marisa Isn't that what you're supposed to call arteestes?

Nick Don't mention those words in this house. Also, look, don't tell jokes about, you know, racist, using those words. I never told you, but Dad's Jewish.

Marisa You never told me he was American. That accent's so oppressive. I see all those massacred Indians. I mean, Americans are the Serbs of the world, aren't they?

Nick What's the good news?

Marisa I haven't slept. I had to take three different trains.

Nick How did you find me?

Marisa I called your mum.

Nick You called my mum!

Marisa I didn't want to call, I wanted to see you.

Nick Well.

Marisa Can't you guess?

Pause.

Nick No.

Marisa The hospital called yesterday, it's definite.

Nick But –

Marisa Didn't you say your dad and Nina couldn't have

children. Now they can have a grandchild.

Nick Don't tell Dad! (*Pause.*) Look, I'm not sure – I have to finish my degree, then I wanted to go to America, do a postgraduate. Dad doesn't have any money any more, I – I mean, you don't have to have it.

Nina comes on.

I need a walk. I'll – I'll – I don't – I don't want it. (*He goes.*)

Marisa You must be Nick's stepmother. Nick says the divorce was very painful for him, maybe that's why he can't be responsible now.

Nina Don't you kids learn sex education in schools?

Marisa Yeah, Nick and I both had an AIDS test.

Tess comes on.

Nina Didn't you take precautions?

Marisa I was sure I couldn't have children. My mother couldn't.

Nina She had you.

Marisa She always said that was a miracle, except she didn't want me.

Nina Wouldn't that suggest –

Marisa I took risks before, nothing happened.

Nina I can't believe this.

Tess It doesn't matter, women make mistakes. I can help you. I know a good clinic. I can make an appointment for you.

April comes on.

Marisa Thanks.

Tess Shall I make one for next week?

Marisa There's plenty of time.

Tess Not that much, you should go soon.

Marisa I know what to do. I'm taking lots of vitamins.

Tess Wait – you're not planning to have it?

Marisa It's a baby.

Tess It's not a baby yet, Marisa.

Nina What did Nick say?

Marisa I don't care. It's not his. I mean it is, but it's mine.

Nina He has years of study ahead of him. On a tiny student grant. You can't expect him to quit and work in a supermarket.

Marisa I can look after myself. The state helps you.

Nina Not any more.

Marisa I'd like to work on a magazine. I like writing.

Tess What are your qualifications?

Marisa I have a GCSE, I can learn to type.

Tess I have girls with firsts from Oxbridge desperate to work as secretaries. They're whizzes at computers.

Marisa I'll work in a pub.

Tess Who's going to look after the baby? Your mother? Didn't you tell Robert she was an alcoholic?

April What are you two trying to do?

Tess Don't meddle, April.

April I'm ashamed of you.

Nina We're trying to look at facts.

April Isn't the reason you haven't had children, Nina, because of an abortion that went septic?

Nina It was a back-street one, you and I marched to make them safe.

April But not to force young women to have them.

Tess April, shut up.

Marisa She's right. You're trying to make me kill my baby, you're child murderers – animal murderers – and –

Nina We're trying to get you to make a sensible decision.

Marisa So I can end up like you, married to ambition, bitter and childless –

Tess We've waited until we could look after our children –

Marisa Looks like you've left it too late –

Tess I don't think so – and at least we won't bring them up on a council estate with a succession of violent men.

Marisa Nick isn't violent.

Nina What makes you think he'll stay with you?

Marisa runs off, crying. Pause.

April I hope you're proud of yourselves.

Nina She can't ruin Nick's life.

April Do you remember Tony? He made me have an abortion, wait until he was divorced for us to have a child. Then his wife got pregnant. I should hate him for ten years of false promises, but I hate her. She was only trying to survive. You're not trying to help Marisa, you simply hate her.

Nina What if Marisa did it on purpose? We fought against that behaviour too.

Tess I don't hate her, I hate stupidity.

April So she has no right to children? I can understand you betraying feminism in your public life but you could at least apply some of it privately.

Tess Who's betrayed feminism? I'm on one of the best magazines around.

April Women's shlock.

Nina I have fun reading it.

Tess It has serious articles.

April Sandwiched between adverts for lipsticks and orgasms.

Tess Orgasms went out of fashion in the eighties – I think the idea was they took too much time –

April Filofaxes, whatever.

Tess They went out of fashion in the nineties, reminded people of the eighties.

April All right, whatever it is.

Tess New Labour. No ideology. Going with the flow. Being gay is stylish. Trees. No cars.

Nina I'm for that.

April I remember what you used to write, the analysis, it was astounding.

Tess *Eve's Pear.* Read by twenty-five people.

April You had one of the best minds – your deconstruction of just the kind of magazine you're editing. How it held up an image of happiness that was unattainable.

Nina Happiness is unattainable, April.

Tess We've had twenty years to discover women don't like serious magazines, they like the ads.

April What can you decide in twenty years? You wanted money, you succumbed to a designer version of yourself – just as you have a designer version of mothers.

Nina You've read the statistics about those mothers, they're frightening.

April The answer isn't forbidding them to have children.

Nina I didn't say that! Or did I? I hope I didn't.

Tess Anyway, we don't say designer, we say label.

April Let me say what I mean: you were corrupted –

Tess Who wasn't?

April You were the standard bearer – not Nina with her songs, not me stuck in my classics, not a lot of other women – you, with your sense of the moment. Listen to you now.

Tess I want a child. I was horrible to Marisa because I was envious, because she has what I want. I could bring it up, I could give it love, and nature goes for an irresponsible girl who only wants a doll. I've been trying for three years, I'm forty years old. I'm in biological recession. I want a child. I've never wanted anything so badly.

Pause.

April Having a child isn't the only purpose of a woman's life. That was our credo.

Tess We were wrong.

34

April Don't say that.

Tess I don't want that conclusion, April. I organized this weekend to avoid it. That's why I asked you. Not just my oldest friends, but my only friends who don't have children. We'd validate each other. Get back some of the passion of our early days when that was the last thing we wanted. Then *she* comes. Nature's mockery. Did you know evolution favours rapists?

Nina There are so many children in the world. Lost. Waiting. Why don't you look into that? I have lots of information.

Tess I couldn't cope with a child who's been abused in different foster homes for years. You have to know your strengths. I want my own child, in here, like her. Lunch must be ready. We have to celebrate.

April Tess, you will get over it. You accept the consequences of your choices. You grieve. You go on.

Tess I wasn't trained for grief. None of our generation was.

Tess and Nina go. April stays. **Paul** *comes on.*

Paul I've read a lot about the sixties generation.

April We came later. We were the women of the seventies, no one talks much about it. (*She leaves.*)

Paul I'm a child of the eighties. I was in a secondary in Antrim when I saw this competition for design. Next thing I knew I was working for the best advertising agency in London. Our clients were the leaders of the country. I got married, I had a kid. I shouldn't be telling you this. I left my job after five years and set up my own company with a partner. I made a million. I was twenty-five. Big house in Suffolk. I was never at the house. I had to get up earlier

35

and earlier to avoid the traffic. I left London later and later to avoid the traffic. Everybody else did the same so I had to get up even earlier. I hated the house anyway. Knick-knacks, the kinds of things my granny had except my wife said they were worth hundreds of thousands, Meissen or something, looked like glass animals to me. One day I was sitting in the traffic, as usual, and I thought, why am I doing this? I couldn't answer. I asked people at work and they said it's because it's what you do, in the eighties, you work hard, you make money, and I thought, why? That night I didn't go home and the next day I filed for divorce, I gave everything to the wife and child and I came here. I worked as a labourer for the local gardener, then I took over. The thing is, I'm really good, I can design gardens, I'm in demand, I could put out a brochure, open up a business, expand, contract out – once you've been bitten by the eighties, it's hard to stop. My friends are riding the recession, waiting for it to be over, so they can be like before. I hope it's never over. I'll vote for the party that doesn't promise an economic recovery.

Paul goes off as Nick and Marisa come on.

Nick There won't be any trains.

Marisa I'll walk.

Nick In your condition?

Marisa Who cares?

Nick I do.

Marisa You don't. You're just like them –

Nick I'm not.

Marisa Always thinking, talking, telling others what to do, you can't feel anything.

Nick I haven't got used to the idea …

36

Marisa See: idea. It has a heart, it wants love.

Nick Yeah …

Marisa It's a miracle, I was really sure I couldn't. You have to give in to life.

Nick Yeah. But now you know you can, maybe later – in a few years –

Marisa You see, just like them, escaping into the future. This is my family. Now.

Nick Yeah, but what about the – well, for it, the future.

Marisa I hate that word. I'm going.

Nick Marisa, stay.

Marisa Why? You don't care.

Nick I do. It's part of me.

Marisa Only if you want it to be.

Nick I do.

Marisa You do?

Nick Yes.

Jamie and Hugh come on.

Jamie We haven't met, I'm a doctor, Tess sent – are you all right?

Marisa I don't believe in doctors, I do herbs.

Jamie That sounds sensible. I heard you weren't feeling well –

Marisa I'm fine. I wouldn't listen to you anyway because I don't trust authority, but I'm fine.

Nick Dad, we're going to make it work together.

37

Hugh Ah – well, if that's what you want.

Marisa Yeah. Would you like us to call it anything. I mean, I thought if it's a boy, maybe Yehudi –

Hugh Mm – I don't know …

April comes on.

Marisa If you don't feel strongly about, about the fact that you're a – I mean, if it's a girl maybe she could have an Indian name, like Sunrise.

Hugh You have a long time to think about that –

April Aurora means sunrise in Latin, that might be better –

Marisa That's good. Is Latin very difficult to learn? Maybe I could become a Latin teacher in my spare time.

April (*to Jamie*) You brought my bag to the guest room, but not yours.

Jamie I left it in the car.

April I'll unpack it for you.

Jamie I called most of my colleagues, the ones who aren't playing golf or tennis. Two of them are leaving the NHS, one's leaving medicine altogether. One of them kept going on about this Shop-a-Doc idea, said we were being turned into a medical Securitate, everybody spying on everybody else.

April You're already giving up. Why don't you get your bag?

Jamie No one seems to know how to fight.

Hugh The trouble with these campaigns is that they exhaust you. Even if you win, it's usually only for a while, then you have to start again. You need support while you're doing it.

Jamie Yes.

Hugh You need a wife, someone intelligent, who knows about these things, like Tess, or April.

Jamie I don't want a family in these circumstances.

April I don't want a family.

Jamie Later, I'd like one.

Hugh Anyway, you need a wife.

April It's too late. The moment's passed.

Beat. April turns away.

Nick Marisa and I don't agree with campaigns. We think that if you lead your life properly as an individual, that pervades the world.

Marisa I've refused to learn to drive.

Hugh You could be right. Maybe progress is the last ideology and that too needs to be exploded. But that would be painful, you're asking for a future where there's no more expansion. You stop with what you have. Zero growth. That's what you young people are into. It's great.

Nick Dad, you're off again.

Marisa I haven't understood a word either, but I'm going to like having you as a father-in-law.

Nick Marisa!

Robert comes on.

Robert I've prepared a surprise for Tess. Nina is going to sing a song she's composed –

Hugh You've got Nina to sing?

Robert Natasha is lighting the candles. Where's Tess?

April She was in the garden looking for her mobile.

Robert I've made the decision. It's a kind of small political gesture. I'm going to play Vershinin. I called the director earlier. He didn't even sound surprised. I'd forgotten how arrogant people are in the theatre, I'm agreeing to starve for a year and he seems to think I should be pleased to have the part. Where has he been in the last fifteen years?

Tess comes on and kisses Robert.

Robert Come and celebrate.

Nina comes on, followed by Natasha with a cake. Nina is singing her song, leading into 'Happy Birthday', which they all sing. Paul comes on with a mobile, which is ringing; he hands it over to Tess with distaste.

Paul Reminds me of my misspent youth, I was going to bury it, but maybe it's important.

April The mobile is the final blow to public space.

Tess (*answering the mobile*) Who? Miss Sehn. Nina, it's for you.

Nina For me? Ah –

April Imagine a march with everyone on their mobiles.

Nina (*answering the mobile*) Yes? What? A little girl … I see. How old is she? Yes, we have everything.

Hugh has begun to listen.

Hugh A little girl …

Nina clicks the phone off.

Nina She's there. She's waiting for us.

40

Robert Who? Where?

Hugh Our little girl …

Tess No …

Nina She's in Eastern Europe. She's not well.

Tess No.

Nina I enquired a year ago. It didn't look possible.

Tess You didn't even say anything.

Nina I couldn't talk about it. I tried, earlier.

Tess And now, on my telephone, no.

April Tess – be generous.

Nina Come with me, Tess, there are so many children.

Tess I don't want some stolen Romanian baby with AIDS. We ran articles on them.

Nina All media stories about adoption are negative. I've done my own research.

Jamie We have had some very sick children from Romania.

Nina It's not Romania.

Robert It's very exciting.

Nina Tess, I mean it, come with us.

Tess I won't, Nina, but I do wish you well, I do. I've decided to go to a fertility clinic. I know of a very good one. I'll call on Monday. I don't want to waste any more time.

Jamie Tess, do you know what you're getting into?

Tess Yes. Now I want to drink to Nina and Hugh.

There's some elderflower water for Marisa.

Nick Dad, does this mean you're going to be a dad again?

Hugh So it seems.

Nick I hope you do a better job this time. Look, I'll give you advice.

Marisa I think it's great news. Weird. But great.

Jamie My hospital has the best paediatric department – well, used to. It may be open for a few months –

April I'll advise you on schools.

Paul I'll plant a tree.

Tess Will you bring her down here?

Mr Hardacre, *a man of eighty, comes on with a suitcase.*

Mr Hardacre Good day. Paul said you needed some tomatoes for the intruder. (*He opens his suitcase and carefully brings out the home-grown tomatoes.*)

Robert Thank you, Mr Hardacre, will you join us?

Mr Hardacre I'm going on my march with my suitcase.

Nick A march? Where?

Mr Hardacre It's my wife. I was born the year the First World War started. My dad survived, but three of my uncles died. Look at this tomato, isn't it beautiful? My wife's father was a Jew from Macedonia, he had a good business in France. When they were rounding up the Jews, this is 1943 now, I was in the RAF, she and her mother escaped. This was her suitcase. I met her in 1949. She taught at the village school here and to this day old pupils come looking for her, I think because she brought an air of history with her. She was such a good teacher, she had a temperament, the children loved it, she used words like art, truth, beauty, not very English, you might say. She always kept her suitcase. She died three years ago just when the war in Eastern Europe started. I watch the television all the time now. And I see them. I think I see her. People with suitcases, walking, walking with their suitcases. I thought we'd never see those images again. Do you remember in Denmark how everybody wore a Star of David as a protest against the Nazis? To say we are all one. This suitcase is my Star of David. I'm going to march with my suitcase every day for the rest of my life. I'm going to protest against history.

He goes. Pause.

Nina Natasha, where are you from?

Natasha Madame, quick, your candles. (*She points to the candles on the birthday cake.*)

Tess Yes. My candles.

Fade.

Act Two

The airport of an Eastern European country. Hugh, Nina and various airport scroungers.

Nina We've been waiting for an hour and forty-five minutes.

   A man approaches them.

Maybe he won't come. Maybe it's a hoax.

Man Taxi? Very good car.

Hugh (*to the man*) We've told you: we're waiting for someone.

Man Maybe he not come.

Hugh (*to Nina*) I spoke to him on the telephone from London – he'll come.

   A woman approaches.

Woman Hotel? Very good room.

Hugh (*to woman*) We have somewhere, thank you. (*to Nina*) Are you sure you want to go through with this?

Woman Where? Where you stay?

Hugh We don't know, it's been arranged –

Nina I suppose you don't.

Woman Best room in the city. Best view of demonstrations.

Hugh No!

The woman goes.

If it's what you want.

Nina What's the point if you don't?

Hugh I have a son. I know it's not the answer to everything.

A man approaches.

Man Currency? Very good terms.

Nina You don't think it's going to work. Fine. Let's go back. There must be flights tonight.

Man Better than bank, better than black market.

Hugh This is Eastern Europe, there is probably only one plane and it's gone. We may need currency, I couldn't get any in London. Let's see it through. (*to the man*) What's the exchange rate?

Man Very good terms.

A woman comes on.

Nina It's not a record contract, you have to want it to happen.

Woman Icon? Very good saint.

Hugh I want it to happen for you. (*to the man*) OK, here's fifty dollars, what do I get?

Nina That's not good enough.

The man grabs the money.

Man Much. Much. I come back. (*He goes.*)

Hugh Wait!

Man Taxi?

Hugh (*to Nina*) I think I've just lost fifty dollars.

Man Taxi?

Woman Saint, makes miracles.

Hugh I'm supposed to be producing three tracks for one of my favourite singers. I've delayed for two weeks to come here, isn't that enough?

A gypsy comes on, begging, with something wrapped like a baby.

Nina Not if you don't want it.

Hugh I said I would help you even if it's a completely crazy idea.

Nina That's a useless attitude.

Hugh (*to the gypsy*) We don't have any local money.

Gypsy I take dollars.

The woman selling icons spits at the gypsy and sends her away.

Woman You need saint protection in this country. Here.

Hugh All right. It's a wonderful adventure. Where is this man?

Two students come on with flowers and hand them to Nina and Hugh. They take them, astounded.

Girl student Welcome.

Boy student We come every evening and now you are here!

Hugh Wait.

Boy student Our director is here too, he is very tired but the joy of seeing you will make him beter. I run to get him.

Nina I think there's a mistake.

Girl student Dahvid, Kyril?

A bookseller spproaches.

Bookseller Books.

Hugh We are Hugh and Nina.

Girl student You are not Dahvid Edgahr and Kyril Churchill, not delegation of United Kingdom theatre?

Hugh My wife's a singer.

Girl student Oh, this is terrible.

Nina hands back the flowers.

Every day for week we come with flowers. With fax and telepphone broken at our drama academy we do not know arrival.

The boy student comes on with a very effete, well-wrapped, fatigued director.

Director C'est avec plaisir que jour après jour nous vous attendons. (*He holds out a delicate hand.*)

Nina Nous ne sommes pas – Je suis une chanteuse.

Director Quel dommage. Ca ne fait rien. Venez voir notre théatre. C'est au milieu de la ville. Les trois Soeurs.

They lead the director out. He waves in a kind of blessing.

Bookseller (*taking out his books*) Agatha Christie. Guide to this country. Greek myths.

Hugh Can I see the guide? (*looking at the book*) It was written in 1968.

Bookseller Classic.

The money-changer comes back on.

Man Here. You count?

Hugh I'm sure it's fine.

Hugh buys the guidebook. A prostitute comes by.

Prostitute Massage?

Nina No thank you.

Prostitute Men only.

Woman Saint. Buy saint.

An old man comes on.

Old man Medals? Uniforms?

Nina What are we going to do?

Man Taxi?

Other man I am also guide. This country is not (*gestures width*), but it is (*gestures depth*). Ancients, Greeks, Romans, Khans, Byzantium, Turkish Yoke, Russian Yoke, now West. I show you ancient monuments and new monument by American democracy.

Woman You cannot sleep in airport, I take you to hotel.

Other woman Saint, you have saint.

Man Taxi! I take luggage now.

Mihail *comes on, breathless. He rushes to Hugh and Nina, shakes their hands as everyone else disperses. He is formally dressed.*

Mihail Hugh, Nina, you are so welcome. I spent all last night in a petrol queue. Two hours before your plane is to land in this country they run out. I abandon the car, I rush to the bus, the bus does not come. Such is our life in the

48

new chaos, but your hotel is booked, we will take a taxi, eat supper, and tomorrow we look for your child.

Nina Where is she?

Mihail That is what we do not yet know.

Hugh We understood she was in a hospital here in the capital.

Mihail She was. But she is now out of hospital. That is good news, no?

Nina Yes, it is, but where is she?

Mihail I think she is not in the capital. This happens.

Nina What's happened?

Mihail Nothing has happened. It can happen a child is here and then somewhere else. Or that we have not understood where she is. I have a good friend at the Ministry of Health, he will find out. And tomorrow you will meet my wife, Eva. Now let us go to the hotel and then to dinner.

Hugh My wife would like to rest.

Mihail We have very good restaurants in this city.

Hugh Thank you, Mihail, but we're both very tired.

Mihail And then the wine is not expensive although it is more expensive than it was. I have arranged a table.

Nina Of course, we'd be delighted. Mihail, I can't stop thinking about the child.

Mihail We will find her.

Nina Tomorrow?

Hugh I have to get back in a few days.

Mihail Do not book your ticket yet. This is a beautiful country. Perhaps tomorrow we go to the mountains.

———

Song.

———

A London clinic. **Dr Glad**, *Tess Robert.*

Dr Glad We can do anything. Have you seen those strange fertility goddesses in the British Museum? Now women have us. You seem to have what we call reduced fertility. Nothing is wrong, but nothing is right. It may be that naughty biological clock for you, Tess. And the twentieth century isn't kind to men with their sperm count. First we'll jolly up your eggs with two weeks of hormones, given to us by nice menopausal women, mostly Italian nuns, that's why it's quite expensive. Then in about two weeks, a little operation. On that day, we'll cream off the best of your sperm, give it a good spin and presto. A nurse will go over all the details with you. You'll have to be examined every other day, so we advise you to give up work. I don't like to give interviews, but you can see me on the television tonight on the six o'clock news, we've performed another miracle. Best of luck. You pay as you go out.

Robert Luck?

Dr Glad Attitude is important. Think positive.

———

Inside a church. Hugh, Nina, **Eva.** *Also some people doing what people do in Eastern churches: crossing themselves, kissing icons, muttering.*

Eva (*to Nina*) What a beautiful face you are, the face of someone who suffer too much. I, too, suffer. You cannot have a child from this country.

Nina We were told we could have a child who was ill. Eva, I want to see her.

Eva My husband says someone from the ministry come, but he cannot. My husband, he is old. His power is – thrown over. And this man, he is gypsy. But I pray and maybe God listens to me.

Mihail comes on.

Mihail I call, he is not there. He must come soon.

Hugh We've been here an hour and a half.

Mihail I am a Marxist but I am proud of our churches. We respected them. It was always a good place for meetings. (*He indicates that no one can listen.*)

Nina It's very beautiful.

Hugh Are you sure this man is coming?

Mihail The church across from your hotel was built by the Russians to remember our help for liberation from the Turkish Yoke. And you will see our monasteries – he lends me a an obligation –

Hugh Owes me a favour –

Mihail Hugh, you will help me with my English.

Eva He will not come.

Mihail He come maybe by a circular road, not to be seen.

Hugh Are we doing anything illegal?

Mihail I am a lawyer, I do not allow that.

Boian comes on. Eva rushes to him and shakes his hand.

Eva You are man of honour, I will light a candle for your good health.

Boian I didn't want to be seen leaving the ministry. Things are difficult, there are so many rumours.

Eva Do not say, see how this poor girl suffers.

Nina What rumours?

Boian People are now so confused and suspicious, they are saying foreigners come to this country to get organs for babies.

Nina How horrible, but I'm sure it's a myth.

Boian This might happen in Romania, not here, but the West lumps all Balkans together. The minister is disturbed and the people are ignorant. And when there are such rumours – I am a gypsy, the only one in the ministry, the only gypsy ever educated abroad – because of Mihail –

Eva It is impossible, I always say.

Mihail This is a difficulty but Boian, is it not surmountable?

Eva No, it is the end.

Nina Do you know where she is?

Boian Not yet. She left hospital three days ago. I will find out where she was sent. And when you visit, you will say you are a delegation from the Red Cross.

Hugh It's not true!

Mihail To prevent rumours. Of course everyone will know the truth.

Nina I can do that. I'll wear glasses.

Boian I will come back in three days, I cannot say the time.

Hugh Listen, in three days –

Mihail (*over*) Boian, we will be here.

Nina Yes.

Boian Three days is very soon.

Nina Do you have a photograph of her?

Boian I saw her when she was in the hospital, she is very beautiful.

Nina What does she look like?

Boian A baby. Now I have to get back.

Eva We brought a little thing, English.

She fetches a carrier bag full of clinking bottles. Boian takes them without a word and leaves.

Eva I knows God hears me. Even under communism, I pray, so I have special relationship.

———

London. Tess in a hospital gown. She is depressed. Dr Glad comes on.

Tess Doctor, I've been waiting for you.

Dr Glad Feeling a little sore? It's the air pumped into the body and the cutting, of course. You know the drill: phone us in two weeks and ask to speak to the nurse.

Tess What do you think?

Dr Glad We found one viable egg. I would have preferred more, but it only takes one. And your husband's sperm looked a little depressed, but I live in hope. Now I have to go and induce one of my babies, we didn't think that would work either.

Tess I've read the statistics, ten per cent, going down to six. That's not very good, is it?

Dr Glad But you could be the lucky one, Tess.

———

The church. Nina, Hugh.

Nina We've been waiting a week. It's freezing in here. It's a beautiful church, but it wasn't meant to be lived in. I need a cup of coffee.

Hugh Do you want to give up?

Nina I suppose you do.

Hugh Let's give it another day. If we don't, you won't forgive yourself. Worse, you won't forgive me.

Nina The songs I could write about waiting –

Hugh We don't have a bad life, Nina. And having a child is a lot of work.

Nina You really don't want this to happen.

Hugh What am I doing here, then?

Nina How do I know? Maybe you want to sign up the church choir.

Hugh All I'm saying is, you won't be able to moon around being selfish.

Nina I see.

Hugh You're self-absorbed, like most artists. I don't mind, I'm used to it, you're not the worst.

Nina I'm not an artist any more. The product's gone, but I'm stuck with the temperament. Or rather you are. What are we doing together in this crazy country? Why did you come?

54

Hugh Because you decided this was your happiness and when you love someone you follow their zigzags.

Nina It's not me you love, it's my first album.

Hugh If you're going to behave like this, I will go back to London.

Nina Hugh, I want to see her. She's there, somewhere, all alone, herself. I feel her presence, but I don't have a face.

Hugh I think it's going to work.

Nina You think God is on our side? Or because it's you? Even Americans don't always get what they want.

Hugh No, but they're better at it. They try harder.

Boian comes on.

Nina Boian!

Boian Have you seen the demonstrations? We think government might have to resign. This would complicate everything.

Hugh Any news?

Boian Yes, I have good news.

Nina She's here!

Boian Not here, but you can drive in a day. Here is the address. Remember you are from the Red Cross. Please do not get me into trouble. This is a bad time.

Boian leaves. Hugh and Nina look at the writing.

Nina We must learn the alphabet.

Eva comes on.

Eva I pray to all the saints, but they look sad.

Nina We have the address!

Eva looks at the paper.

Eva Holy Mother of God, it is a terrible town. The people are black. Small. My husband has a heart attack in that town. I was here, in the capital, I took bus, all night, bumping, turning, I came to hospital room and there was other woman. How I suffer. But my husband was dying. I forgive. I prayed, he lived. But he has weak heart. If he goes back to that town, he can have other heart attack. It is too much, he is old, I know you suffer, you want child, but this town can attack my husband's heart. Please, perhaps tomorrow you go back to London?

———

Hugh, Nina.

Hugh We drove west to east on an empty road. Soft mountains, rich plains, sudden pollution, a valley of roses, then emptiness. When we tell her the story we will say this: we did our best to play the part of Red Cross officials well. We looked at every baby in the room, we checked the cots, all very clean, and then Mihail whispered to us, there, there, and thrust a baby in Nina's arms.

Nina Light, thin. I felt delicate bones through my fingers. Another baby was quickly thrust in the other arm and Hugh took a picture. The other baby vanished and I looked at her. I will say to her: It was not like the fairy-tales. You did not look up and smile. Faces meant nothing to you: food came from white coats and I wasn't wearing one. But I held you. So light. I held you.

Mihail We leave now. Give her to me.

Nina No.

Mihail They will suspect, Nina. You have to.

Nina No.

Mihail We have to go.

Nina Please. No. (*She bursts into tears.*)

Mihail She is crying too.

———

The hotel room. Hugh, Nina, Mihail and Eva are singing. They have been drinking a lot.

Eva And the words are – how to say, a girl, a girl, she will go, Mihail –

Mihail A girl went out early one morning for water, a young man said to her, stay and talk, they sat and talked, dusk fell and the moon smiled.

Nina And my child came into being …

Mihail We have many great poets too –

Eva Listen: Mother how I misses you now I goes far away. It is better in our language.

Mihail The communists preserved all the poets' houses, one day we go and see –

Hugh How soon can we get her transferred to a home in the capital? Tomorrow?

Mihail Maybe … Maybe the day after …

Nina We need to get her back to England.

Mihail Patience, Nina, there are many horse jumps.

Hugh Hurdles.

Mihail You are decided? I know it was only five minutes –

Hugh We're decided.

Nina Yes.

Mihail This is a beautiful child –

Nina Isn't she?

Eva She is too thin. And her nose.

Nina It's a baby nose, it's beautiful.

Eva And her ear –

Hugh You're sure you can get her transferred?

Eva And her legs – very thin –

Nina That's why I need to get her back and get her on a proper diet immediately.

Mihail He who goes slowly goes fast, as we say. First we get her to the capital, where I know people.

Eva You did, Mihail, now they don't know you.

Mihail We did many good things, Eva, universal education, health, people do not forget – and later bad things, but we wished to do right.

Eva I do not like politics.

Mihail Eva came from a rich family, I was very poor.

Eva He was youngest lawyer ever. I was teener, sixteen.

Mihail I have been a happy man.

Eva They confiscate everything of my family.

Mihail Now you get it back and I help some children –

Eva You like power, Mihail, like alcohol.

Mihail Eva, do not say these things –

Eva It is the truth.

Mihail We communists thought we had the truth. Now I know truth is not fixed, it is not Platonic ideogram, it moves with history. I will not let them make me believe I am evil because that is the new truth. (*He bangs his fist.*) No one will tell me capitalism is truth.

Eva You see, politics is bad for heart.

Mihail In the capital, every taxi driver charges different fare. In front of your hotel, Hugh, the most expensive. They beat up any driver who does not belong to hotel mafia.

Eva You had Mafia too.

Mihail It was Mafia with ideals. I told the government when they were bad.

Eva That was very stupid. We had terrible times.

———

London. Tess, Robert.

Robert It's one minute to twelve, we can call.

Tess Ready? (*She dials on her phone.*) Hello, it's Tess Warner. (*Pause.*) I see. Yes. Well, it's not your fault.

Robert It didn't work.

Tess shakes her head.

I'm sorry.

Tess That's not good enough.

Robert goes to her.

Don't touch me.

Robert Tess …

Tess We'll have to do it again, that's all.

Robert No.

Tess The odds diminish as you keep going.

Robert We've just spent five thousand pounds. It's not even that, I can't stand to see you doing this to yourself.

Tess I'm giving myself a chance for happiness.

Robert Tess, the drugs, the anaesthetic, this waiting. I don't want to make love to two tubes at once, so they can split off the cream or whatever they do – with a porn magazine in front of me. You need to go back to work.

Tess I'm not interested.

Robert Life goes on.

Tess Not mine.

Robert That sounds stupid, but it does. We must live. I fell in love with an independent, intelligent woman. Only two months ago I'd call you and hardly get past your secretary.

Tess You have your revenge.

Robert I'm proud of you. I don't want a mother for my children.

Tess You can always find one when you do.

Robert I have to go back to rehearsals. I got the afternoon off, but I was asked to be back this evening. I'm sorry.

Tess You'll have to take a television, we're out of money.

Robert My contract is for the year.

Tess Break it.

Robert It's the first time for years I've enjoyed myself. It's difficult, precise, strange and also familiar. What you want in a part. It's terribly sad, and yet, the acceptance of life, the slit of hope – read it, Tess.

Tess I can't concentrate. Can't you do some ads?

Robert You know I won't.

Tess That's ridiculous, politicians do them, even magazine editors. What's the difference between an ad and a drama anyway? It's all the selling of dreams.

Robert If you no longer know that, you –

Tess What? Go on.

Robert I have to go to rehearsals.

Tess It's easy for you. You can escape into your romantic Vershinin, not think about anything –

Robert It's my work. I'm already late. I do understand.

Tess No, you don't.

Robert No, I don't. Come to rehearsals, you can sit in the coffee room.

Tess Just what I need: a grimy room full of obsessed actors.

Robert Call an old friend, Nina, April, someone at work.

Tess Nina's still out of the country, April thinks IVF is a male conspiracy to sell women drugs, the women at work have children, I have no one – it should be you –

Robert Tess, acting may be a useless profession, but people work hard at it. I can't ring and say I'm not coming.

Tess You'll be all right, you can always play King Lear.

Robert I won't be asked if –

Tess But what am I going to do for the next twenty years?

Pause.

I'm making an appointment for next week.

Robert I won't do it.

Tess You have to. I'll sell the house in the country. One more time. Otherwise – we're nothing.

Robert How can you say that?

———

Eastern Europe. The hotel. Hugh and Nina are packing. Nina looks at a few items of baby clothes. They are both dejected.

Nina I'll leave them in the room. A cleaner will find them.

Hugh We can try somewhere else.

Nina I'm not going through this again.

Hugh looks out the window.

Hugh Look, another demonstration.

Nina ignores this.

Nina I don't understand. First it was the next day, then a week's delay, then another week, now they don't even bother to say.

Hugh Eva said she would come and say goodbye.

Nina I don't want to see her.

Pause.

You didn't hold her.

Hugh There are other children. I promise, we'll look.

Nina I don't want another child. I want the child I held.

Hugh takes a photograph out of his pocket and looks at it.

Nina You'll never understand.

Hugh is keeping himself from tears. Nina notices this.

Hugh …

Hugh When it was an abstraction, I didn't – I thought it was a pretty loopy idea. Then there's a child … and she even looks like you …

He is really crying now. Nina holds him.

Nina Hugh … why didn't you say? Don't cry. I can't bear it. Somebody has to hold the world firm. How can I be saying this? I'm going to get us some vodka.

Nina rushes out. Hugh puts the picture back in his pocket. Eva comes on.

Eva You pack, I am so truly sorry, where is Nina? I know you think we cheat and lie, but it is Mihail. He thinks he can do things but he is nobody now and everyone, how do you say, overflow with fear. Before we were afeared but we knew of what. Now … You come at wrong political time. Everyday more expensive. And we have only pension. Look out there, politicians cannot agree government. The Turks hold balance, but if they hold power, we have war. I would like to come to England. A ticket, is not expensive? I clean houses. And the snows come. Even if baby will come to capital you cannot do anything when snows are here. And my husband, he is more fragile of heart. Maybe I die of cold.

Mihail comes on, out of breath, sinks down.

Mihail I did not want to telephone. (*He pauses for breath.*)

Eva He is dying.

Mihail I have run.

Eva Call ambulance!

Mihail Hugh –

Eva Water. Quick. Do not speak Mihail, you will die.

Eva covers Mihail's mouth with her hand; he manages to take it away.

Mihail I am so happy.

Eva He is seeing paradise. He is a good man, God will forgive the communism.

Mihail She is here.

Eva Yes, I pray to Mother of God. Now she take him.

Eva crosses herself. Mihail catches his breath.

Mihail Nina. Where is Nina?

Eva Always the younger woman, but I forgive. Hugh, call ambulance.

Mihail The little girl is here. She came last night.

Eva You see, I pray, and now God takes pity of mother, I always knew.

Mihail We can see her. I even told big capitalist Mafia taxi downstairs to wait.

Eva Where is Nina? Maybe she commit suicide.

Mihail Today we celebrate, tomorrow real work. You have passports, police records, medical records, accountant letter, good character certification, letter from psychologist, then the social report, I get all translated – yes and marriage certificate, birth certificate, your divorce permit, you have? Photographs of house, name and birth of parents, you have.

Eva Mihail, stop, you get brain tumour.

Hugh It's all here.

Mihail This is good, I am impressed.

Hugh I studied law before becoming a record producer.

Mihail You never said.

Eva Hugh is modest American and all your life you say terrible things about Americans.

Hugh It's all right, so do I.

Nina comes on. She is carrying a bottle one-quarter full of vodka and is very drunk.

Nina I seem to have drunk most of this. I was talking to the prostitutes in the foyer –

Mihail Nina, Nina. Your little girl is waiting for you.

Nina takes it in.

Nina She's here?

Eva We stop at church and thank God.

Mihail Afterwards, Eva –

Nina I'm so drunk, what will she think?

————

London. Dr Glad, Tess.

Dr Glad Nature is cruel: you were born with a finite number of eggs and now they're used up or old. I would say try one more time, twice, you might twist my arm and try three times, four, even five, but after that we need to take the next step.

65

Tess What's that?

Dr Glad We use a younger woman's eggs. The success rate zooms up. And we can still use your partner's sperm, we like to include the chaps in all this.

Tess The child won't have my genes …

Dr Glad No, but you'll breastfeed, it'll have your antibodies. I'll put your name down, there's a two-year waiting list –

Tess Two years!

Dr Glad You can jump the queue if you find your own donor. You might have a friend –

Tess There all in the same position I'm in.

Dr Glad Someone at work …

Tess It's a lot to ask …

Dr Glad It is such an altruistic gesture, many women might enjoy it if they knew about it.

Tess Is it expensive?

Dr Glad Double the trouble, double the cost, my secretary can go over that with you, she's been with me for fifteen years, she knows more than I do. No money must be exchanged between the women.

Tess It's dangerous for them?

Dr Glad No more than for you, high doses of hormones, some danger of overstimulation, we monitor very closely. We like to match hair colour and skin.

Tess What about –

Dr Glad Intelligence? That must be left to your husband's genes. Now I must give evidence to an ethics committee, they are so rigid. We're at the forefront of science. You ought to write an article.

Tess And what if that doesn't – work?

Dr Glad A very nice woman the other day had some extra embryos she was willing to give, and there you go, a happy couple were able to adopt an embryo. Before we get to that we would suggest different sperm, we have very nice donors, all nationalities, Jewish, anything you need. And once we don't have to deal with your eggs, Tess, there's no age limit. We can go on for years.

———

The hotel. Nina.

Nina I know only one myth that sings of a mother's love for her daughter. The goddess of the earth, Demeter, loses her daughter to Hades, god of the underworld. In her grief, she blights the crops, famine descends on earth. Diplomatic shuttle on Olympus, a deal is struck: Demeter is allowed her daughter back for two-thirds of the year, but for one-third, Persephone deserts her for the under-world. Demeter mourns her absence by covering the earth with the bleakness of winter.

We don't have the daughter's version. We only know of Demeter's joy when her daughter is by her side, her grief when she's absent. Do I think of this myth because my daughter was absent for the first six months of her life? Because I see her for only one third of the day? I know how fragile is the gift of her presence. And when I cannot hold her, the world goes dark, wintry.

Hugh comes on.

Hugh How did it go?

Nina I held her. I walked up and down in that little office

67

and talked to her. I told her we would be in England soon. She still won't meet my gaze, but she seemed comfortable, almost happy. And so am I. You?

Hugh We picked up the papers from the translators, queued for hours to get every single page stamped. Bureaucracy must make them feel they still have government. I had to call London again. I think I've lost the job.

Nina I'm sorry.

Hugh It's not just the job, it's my reputation. How will we bring up this child?

Nina All right. I'll do the album. As soon as we get back.

Hugh That, Nina, makes me happy.

Nina I'll use some of the music we've heard here. I have to do something for the family. I want to.

Hugh There's something about this country – I'm falling in love again.

Nina I didn't know you'd fallen out of love – you were very polite about it. Why didn't you say?

Hugh Isn't that when you can't talk? At least, men can't.

Eva and Mihail come on.

Eva We cannot do it.

Nina What's wrong now?

Mihail Please, Eva, sit. Good evening, Hugh and Nina, you are well? Perhaps we have some coffee and chocolate cake, yes?

Hugh What's happened?

Mihail We are very worried about the child.

Nina So am I. She needs to get out of that home.

68

Eva She is very ill. Mihail, he is communist, but he has honour, he will not give you very ill child.

Nina She is not very ill.

Hugh We understood your laws would only allow us to have a child who was ill.

Mihail That is the law. It is a good law if the child is a little ill, but if she is very ill it is bad and we cannot do it.

Eva Your heart breaks, Nina, I am mother, I have experience.

Nina I know I can make her well.

Mihail You would not forgive us later – if something terrible happened.

Eva She is so weak.

Nina Of course she is. She needs a home, love, good food.

Hugh You told us originally she had been taken to hospital with gastroenteritis, and that it was not very serious.

Mihail That is what we thought.

Hugh Well?

Mihail The director of the home thinks she is more ill. I am not a doctor, I do not understand.

Eva She is losing weight, any mother can see that.

Nina So would any child with that brew they feed her. Hugh, let's call Jamie right now and get him over here to examine her.

Mihail Nina, Nina, patience, we have good doctors here.

Nina Call a doctor in, then. Now.

Hugh Let's get the consultant who looked after her in hospital.

Mihail If I arrange that, and the consultant says she is very ill, you must promise you will not insist.

Nina I don't care how ill she is. I can cope.

Eva No, Nina, you cannot, you are a nervous.

Mihail Hugh, I must warn you, if she is ill I will not help you. Forgive me.

Nina Then we'll manage without you.

Hugh Nina!

Nina I didn't mean that. Actually, I did. I can't let her go. (*She bursts into tears.*)

Mihail You have promise of happiness and we snatch it away, but you have other promises, Nina.

Eva We find other child, with something tiny wrong.

Hugh and Nina No!

Eva She smiles when she sees Hugh, she likes men. I cry. Nina, do you have handkerchief?

Nina No! I don't.

———

London. Robert, Tess.

Robert Today, I tried playing Vershinin as a pompous dreamer. It didn't work. What's difficult is to find that belief in the future, it's the most dated part of the play.

   Pause. Tess doesn't respond.

Chekhov knew things were going badly. It must have been his act of courage to keep faith with humanity – most of

70

us don't have that faith. (*Pause.*) The director wondered how much evidence you needed to stop being a humanist – you're not interested.

Tess You never used to talk about rehearsals.

Robert I didn't need to.

Tess What does that mean?

Robert You used to come home full of the people you'd met, articles you'd commissioned.

Tess Mm.

Robert When are you going back to work?

Tess I'm not supposed to have any stress.

Robert Tess, you have to work.

Tess Why?

Robert Partly to pay the mortgage and partly to come home and tell me what you did all day.

Tess I can tell you what I do every single day. I walk down the street and leer at women. Which one has the good eggs? There's an exhausted twenty-year-old with three brutalized children. Shall I tell her I'll get her out of her rut in exchange for her eggs – but what kind of genes does she have? I spot a young mother in a book store, perfect: brainy eggs. She goes to the feminist section, she'll wonder why my only identity is motherhood. There's a foreign student. I fantasize about kidnapping her. I wouldn't have pity. I sit on a park bench like a flasher. Women used to be my sisters. They're objects: egg vessels. Now you know.

Robert Tess …

Tess I will find somebody.

71

Robert If you don't?

Tess I can't stop now.

Robert The agents called today, they want us to drop the price of the house again.

Tess It won't be worth selling.

Robert Then we have to stop. You're going to lose your chance of becoming Editor.

Tess We'll remortgage. If you'd only taken that television – that was so irresponsible.

Robert To what? Your madness.

Tess It's mad to do theatre these days, you've said it yourself.

Robert It's what I love. I've even got my confidence back, in it, in myself, in the worth of it all.

Tess It's not very significant, is it?

Robert What does that mean?

Tess Putting your life on hold for a few hundred people a night.

Robert That is my life.

Tess So you wreck ours.

Robert I'm not wrecking it, you have. I don't recognize you, it's like living with a junkie. Always waiting for the next fix, of hormones, of hope. What do you think it's like?

Tess What do you think it was like living with you last year when you were unemployed and despising everything? I tried to feel it with you –

Robert It wasn't a situation of my making.

Tess Nor is this. Don't you want a child?

Robert Not that badly, no. I want you –

Tess You mean my earning capacity?

Robert I want to go out with you, I want to make love to you for the pleasure of it, I can't even remember what that's like.

Tess Is that all you can think about?

Robert It used to be something you enjoyed.

Tess turns away. Pause.

I have to go over my lines.

Tess Are there any young actresses in the company?

Robert The one playing Irina. Would you like to meet the company? They'd love to see you.

Tess You could ask her – you could ask her if she would like to donate her eggs.

Robert I can't believe this.

Tess What's wrong? Why shouldn't she? She could do it when she's not working. Ask her.

Robert These hormones are wrecking your brain.

Tess What a disgusting thing to say.

Robert Well, I must be a shit.

Tess If it weren't for your sperm, I'd leave you.

Robert Perhaps that would be best.

Tess What are you saying?

Robert Look, I have to go over the lines, some of the speeches are rather convoluted.

Tess Repeat what you said just now – repeat those lines.

Robert shakes his head.

———

Dr Attanasov, *Mihail, Eva, Hugh, Nina.*

Dr Attanasov She was admitted to this hospital with a very high fever and severe dehydration caused by gastroenteritis. She was also suffering from anaemia and a general failure to thrive. We diagnosed a lactose intolerance, and recommended a diet without milk. I have checked the records and spoken to my colleagues: there was no internal damage. There is no reason why the child should not be perfectly healthy.

Hugh and Nina embrace.

I will write a report to the Ministry of Health.

Hugh No, don't do that.

Beat.

Mihail Is there not a possibility that this condition will recur? She could have a high fever again? I am not a doctor … Dehydration, that is terrible, I know about that.

Dr Attanasov She will be healthy. It is best to keep her on a diet without milk.

Mihail A correct diet, that is very difficult in a home. We do not know what will happen with the economic situation.

Dr Attanasov The medical standards of our homes are excellent.

Hugh She is losing weight.

Eva She is thin, thin, thin, every day more.

Dr Attanasov I have her graph, yes, she is under the normal, but I have seen much worse.

Nina Doctor, you diagnosed a general failure to thrive, what causes that?

Dr Attanasov It could be sadness.

Nina And the love of two parents could cure that?

Dr Attanasov Yes, but that is not a medical fact.

Nina Isn't it?

Mihail Doctor, these kind people came here because they heard this child was ill.

Dr Attanasov Yes ...

Mihail Doctor, the law will only allow this child out on humanitarian grounds – a small word in the law, but in the heart a large one.

Dr Attanasov I understand, but I cannot write a false report.

Mihail Of course, we would not ask that.

Hugh We love this child.

Nina Doctor, I think we can guarantee she will thrive.

   Pause.

Dr Attanasov I can say she was brought to hospital in a critical condition and that we suspected pancreatic insufficiency or some form of immunodeficiency. If no one asks me further questions, I will not have to answer them.

Nina Thank you, doctor.

Dr Attanasov Please understand that if I am asked, I will have to give the results of our tests. But next week, I am not much at my desk. Goodbye. I count on you to make this child happy.

———

Song.

———

Statelov, *an old lawyer, comes on. He kisses Nina's hand and clicks his heels at Hugh. He and Mihail embrace.*

Statelov I take you into Ministry of Justice. I am supervisor of files. Very important position. Everyone knows Mr Statelov. I have friends in the courts too. Do you know Dunhill pipes? I have three. Maybe you send me more? I also have Great Dane. His name is Free Market.

Mihail I thought his name was Collective.

Statelov That was many years ago, terrible name.

Mihail Is it?

Statelov History, my friend, moves and we move with it. History moves very fast in Eastern Europe. Government will fall any day. Then who knows who rises, Turks, gypsies, worse: Jews. Poor Mihail, he move too slowly and now no one likes him. Only Statelov can get you the letter you need. Madame, you are most attractive.

Nina Thank you. It's so kind of you to help us.

Statelov kisses Nina's hand again and leaves.

Hugh Do we have to deal with him?

Mihail (*angry*) Do you know what this costs me?

Eva He was much in love with me, I think he still feels.

———

Robert and Tess. Robert brings a suitcase. A silence.

Robert You could still come.

Tess What for?

Robert Because it's East Germany, Tess, and it's interesting. Look out there, there's a world, remember? You used to be part of it. (*He stops himself.*) What's the point?

   Pause.

I don't know where I'll stay when I come back, but you have the touring schedule. I'll call.

Tess You don't have to.

Robert What a way to end.

Tess Isn't it.

   Pause.

I remember at the beginning I'd wait up for you, and you'd walk in still quite high after a performance and I'd think, he's mine, my man. I'd pretend to have done something else all evening. Really, I'd been waiting for you.

Robert What happened?

Tess It wasn't every eveneing. I was very busy.

Robert Come back to me. Come back to yourself.

Tess This is myself. You don't like it.

Robert No, I'm sorry, I hate it.

   Pause.

I'm sorry.

Tess There we are.

Robert Yes.

Tess You're going to miss your plane.

Robert turns away.

Robert I don't know what to say to you.

Tess There's nothing to say.

———

Statelov, Nina, Hugh, Eva, Mihail.

Statelov My friends, I work so hard, charming Madame. I have done well.

Mihail You have the letter from the Minister of Justice?

Statelov Ah no, not the letter. I am sorry, that is impossible.

Hugh That's what we need!

Statelov I have the promise of the letter. But my friend wants letter from Minister of Health first.

Mihail We cannot get it, you know that. It is the Deputy Minister of Health who insisted on this law that makes adoption nearly impossible. But we do not need a letter from her, only from Ministry of Justice. Without that, we cannot bring the case to court. I explained all this.

Statelov I have the promise of the letter from Minister of Justice.

Nina Isn't that enough?

Hugh Promises don't hold water in a courtroom.

Statelov I work very hard, here is my bill.

Mihail looks at it.

Mihail This is criminal.

Statelov Western prices. I am lawyer.

Mihail This is communist country!

Statelov I was never communist.

Mihail You worked for the government.

Statelov I was not communist in my heart, like you. You would not speak to me in the street. Now I help.

Mihail These people do not have that kind of money

Statelov I take some off if you send Dunhill pipes.

Mihail I am a Marxist, but now I want to go pray. I am a tired man. I have failed my country. I have failed you.

Nina I'm staying in the country. I'll go to the home every day.

Eva You cannot: they will become suspicious.

Hugh Surely everyone knows what we are doing by now. It's above board, isn't it?

Mihail Above board, that means – Ah, I understand. It is legal, I assure you, but nothing in our country is above board. In yours, yes? (*He leaves.*)

Statelov These communists, they fail the world.

Pause.

Eva Nina, I think to myself, this Deputy Minister, she is woman, you are woman.

Nina ignores her.

And you, Hugh, are a gentleman, women like that.

Statelov I look much like English gentleman when I smoke my Dunhill pipe.

Eva Mr Statelov, are you afraid of the Ministry of Health?

Statelov Statelov knows no fear.

Eva All my life I apologize to Mihail, to communists. He is unfaithful too. I am for personalism. I say, politics, enough. I am ideologist of heart. You all follow me. I say: let us storm the barricades.

———

Song.

———

The Ministry of Health. **Dr Romanova** *comes in. Eva bars Romanova's way.*

Eva Dr Romanova, we throw ourselves down before your feet: we cry pity for the poor mother. (*She gets down on her knees.*) You are a woman, you understand woman's pain. Listen and your great heart has been moved. Nina: speak. Sing!

Eva tries to drag Nina down on her knees.

Statelov Allow me to introduce myself. Mr Statelov. I am inspector of files for Ministry of Justice. Also, my wife's sister is a friend of your husband's brother's wife. They went to school –

Eva shoves Statelov aside.

Eva They love the little girl so much. Every night, Madame Sehn falls into tears, how they flow, if you seen, you who have mother's heart will also have flow. I have flow.

Hugh Dr Romanova, we are trying to adopt a child in this country. She has been ill. We want to give her a home.

Nina All our love.

Statelov The Ministry of Justice where I am inspector will hand over letter, but they need one from you. They say I may soon be transferred to Ministry of Health. I am very thorough.

Dr Romanova looks at him coldly.

Dr Romanova You know the law. We do not allow children under one year to leave the country and even then –

Hugh In this case, there are humanitarian grounds.

Eva Look how humanitarian these parents are. And the English gentleman. A saint. He gives up work, career, he is famous musician, how many woman have husband, father like that. I cry.

Nina We love this child, she will be well looked after, as happy as we can make her –

Eva And Nina sings so beautiful, like this – (*She begins to sing.*) Nina, sing.

Dr Romanova That is not necessary. The pressure against adoption, you must know, comes from abroad.

Eva She is ill, she has terrible cough like this. (*She coughs.*)

Nina Dr Romanova, I believe it is necessary for us to take this child back to England without delay. I am not a doctor, but I feel, I know, she will give up, just give up, from lack of love, you must understand.

Dr Romanova Yes –

Eva Pity for the mother and child in this world full of pain. Pity for –

Dr Romanova Enough, please. (*Beat.*) I will write the letter.

Eva embraces Dr Romanova's skirt.

81

Eva You are sage.

Dr Romanova Please do not tell people in England it is easy to adopt in this country.

Hugh It would not be possible to say that. Thank you.

Nina I promise we will do all we can for her.

Nina bursts into tears. Eva cries too.

Dr Romanova Come back at two.

Statelov Today.

Dr Romanova Tomorrow.

Statelov But if the government –

Dr Romanova Tomorrow at two. Goodbye.

————

Mihail It is fashionable to condemn the twentieth century and make us the villains of the piece. I confess terrible things were done, in our name, and by us. And yet, we had ideals. Now I see the ideals are gone. People talk freely, but only about money. Idealism has turned on its head, everyone looks after himself in a world of chaos. I am an old man. I have known fear but now I see people suffer the greatest fear of all: fear of the future. I loved the future, even if I feared the present, with its sudden disgraces. I refuse to recant. I still believe in history. Now, it will be in the hands of the children, possibly most of all, these cross-border children I have helped to get out. Born in one country, loved and raised in another, I hope they will not descend into narrow ethnic identification, but that they will be wilfully international, part of a great European community. I hope they will carry on history with broad minds and warm hearts. They have the complexity from their childhood: change, migration and indifference and uncertainty came to them early. Now, cherished, secure, educated. Is it unfair of me to place the responsibility of history onto them? We must not go into the next century with no ideal but selfishness.

———

The courthouse. Everyone wrapped in coats. Mihail, Statelov, Boian, Eva, Hugh, Nina.

Nina Now I understand Dickens. We've been waiting five hours.

Mihail Ours must be the last case.

Boian We are lucky to have letters. The government will announce resignation at two o'clock this afternoon. There will be new ministers.

Statelov Only because of me do we get this hearing. Otherwise, until after holidays: court takes five weeks.

Hugh We could leave tomorrow.

Mihail Not tomorrow, Hugh. The judgement must be lodged in the court for a week to allow for an appeal.

Nina What appeal? From whom?

Mihail That is the law.

Hugh Ask the judge to waive the mandatory week, explain the situation.

Boian I will represent Ministry of Health, I will confirm urgency.

Nina Boian, how can we thank you?

Boian Tell your child a gypsy help you. One day when my children need connection, they find your child or grandchild and call on ethnic friendship.

Mihail Anyway, you have to apply for passport for the child. That takes three weeks.

Hugh I'll get it in a day.

Mihail Even in America you do not have passport in a day.

Eva You cannot even be sure the court rules in our favour.

Hugh We have the letters, the papers are in order.

Eva Mihail does not think so.

Hugh What do you mean? Mihail?

Eva Mihail, do you have ear attack?

Mihail I did not want to worry you, Hugh, but I could not go to official translators. So the court could refuse to accept papers.

Nina No.

Hugh Why didn't you use the official translators?

Mihail They require a stamp from our embassy back in England, but that would take six months, a year.

Hugh You mean our papers are illegal?

Mihail They are legal. They are not official.

Statelov They're calling us.

Eva I pray to God to help us

Nina So do I.

Eva crosses herself and, after a moment, so does Nina.

————

Hugh The court case, solemn, brief, was almost an anti-climax. Our petition was read out. We were asked if we understood what we doing. Whether the prosecutor noticed or chose to ignore the irregularity of the papers, we'll never know. I was beginning to discover that once you had people on your side, the law was upheld but happily twisted. We were given our child. (*Pause.*) The prosecutor agreed to waive the mandatory week. The next day was the last working day before the holidays began. At ten o'clock we picked up the judgement and ran to the court cashier to pay for use of the photocopying machine. Suddenly, she disappeared. A long queue was forming.

Where's the cashier?

Mihail Maybe in the bathroom, maybe at lunch. It is festival season.

Hugh I'm going to check out the bathrooms and pull her out.

Mihail You cannot.

Hugh Let's get this copied somewhere else.

Mihail Where? I am embarrassed for my country, it is because of people like her we are in such a mess. We all have important business, she does not care.

Hugh I'm going to use the photocopier without paying.

Mihail That is against the law.

The woman comes on, a bottle of wine in her hands.

Please, we are very grateful if we can copy these papers.

Hugh We've been waiting an hour!

The woman just stares and slowly focuses.

Woman How many pages?

Mihail Twelve.

The woman counts them, very slowly.

Hugh We told you: twelve!

Woman I make sure. You are English? It is very wet in your country.

Hugh We photocopied the judgement. We took a taxi to the notary. He stamped every page. We now had to get a new birth certificate.

A man comes on with papers.

Man I cannot issue a new birth certificate.

Hugh But –

Man The child was not born in the capital. You must go to the town where she was born.

Mihail The holidays begin tomorrow.

The man nods. A clerk approaches and looks at the papers and a small photograph.

Clerk (*to Hugh*) This is your baby?

Hugh nods. The two men look, others approach, the picture is passed round.

Very beautiful.

Nods all round.

You take her to England?

Hugh I'm trying.

Woman This is good, this is good thing you do.

Hugh What are we going to do without a birth certificate?

Clerk You are sure she wasn't born in capital?

Hugh Of course I'm sure. Look, it says here.

Clerk People make mistakes.

Man I do not remember where my children born. Too much brandy.

Mihail Do you know, I remember now this child was born in my house. That is in the capital. Here is my address.

Clerk I knew there was mistake.

Man You will swear to that?

Mihail Yes. How could I forget such a thing?

Man Then we can proceed.

Hugh We arrived at the passport office twenty minutes before it closed for the holidays.

Man I need the birth certificate, good, and then you must sign here and your wife signs here.

Hugh My wife isn't here.

   Pause.

Man Are you sure? This is a big room. Perhaps she is leaning behind that pillar.

Hugh No, she – oh.

Mihail (*over him*) Yes, she is not feeling well and she is leaning behind a a pillar.

Man That will explain why her handwriting is a little different. Now I will go out of this room to get a glass of water for your wife and you will ask her to sign, yes?

Hugh I forged Nina's signature and we were given our daughter's passport as the bells rang for evening mass.

Eva and Nina come on, singing.

Mihail Nowhere in the world do you get a passport in a day. I am proud of my country.

Hugh All the flights are booked because of the skiing holidays. I said it was a humanitarian emergency and they agreed to bump off two skiers. I hope they don't mind.

Eva No, they are German.

Nina You are a hero.

Nina and Hugh embrace.

Hugh Without you, Mihail –

Mihail I climbed the hills, but Eva conquered the mountain.

They embrace Eva.

Mihail Hugh, I have not told you –

Nina Then don't.

Mihail When you arrive at Heathrow, you may be arrested. Sadly, England does not recognize our laws.

Hugh I can't believe it, after all this?

Mihail You will have the child with you. You will deal with England.

Nina I will deal with them.

Eva Before you were poor bird, now you are lioness, true mother. But Nina, no more peace, always thoughts of your child, now you truly suffer.

Nina As long as she is happy.

Eva So many worries. And look out the window: the snows come. Maybe you cannot leave at all.

Act Three

Six months later. A dressing room in a northen provincial theatre. Robert is taking off his Vershinin clothes. Tess comes in.

Robert I didn't know you were in ... did you see Nina and Hugh?

Tess They're coming ... (*Pause.*) It's your last night –

Robert It's gone fast. (*Pause.*) How are you?

Tess As well as can be expected ... You?

Robert shrugs.

You were very good. I understand why it's been so important. What will you do now?

Robert Wait until I'm offered something else I really want to do. That could be a long wait.

Tess I've put the flat on the market.

Robert You haven't gone back to work?

Tess shakes her head.

Tess ...

Tess I know – there's a world out there. Do you remember the articles I commissioned about the domestic side of war? No one did it before me.

Robert That was brilliant.

Tess Nick is here, I want to speak to him. I've written to Marisa. She's had a baby boy.

89

Robert Ah –

Tess She hasn't answered: I've asked if she would donate her eggs. I know I was horrible to her, but that was a year ago, I'm sure she'll understand.

Robert Tess –

Tess I'll try it once more, no, three times. Then I'll stop.

Pause.

Robert If you want me to come and give you – you know, sperm, no strings attached.

Tess Part of the problem was your sperm. I'm going to use a donor, it's younger, the clinic is very selective.

Robert I see.

Pause.

Tess Well …

Robert Why don't you stay the night?

Tess No.

Robert I miss you. Don't you ever feel – we could go back? Accept what has happened, go on, maybe not be completely happy, but – I don't know – live –

Tess That's fine for the three sisters, they come to terms with their lives, but this is the twentieth century. I won't accept defeat.

Nick comes on.

Nick That was – well, they're all a bit desperate, aren't they, those sisters? And Marisa wouldn't approve of you. She said to say hello, she's at home with the baby, he's got a cold.

Tess How is she?

90

Nick She's finding it hard –

Tess Did she get my letter?

Nick I got it, I read it. She's been too busy to open her post and she was a little depressed after the baby. I thought it was going to be a good wishes letter.

Tess Did you show it to her?

Nick No. I wouldn't let her do it.

Tess Isn't that up to her?

Nick She's the mother of my child. You say it's safe, but those drugs haven't been around that long and we feel she should breastfeed for at least two years anyway. Don't you think you should forget about all that? Your letter sounded – well – desperate.

Tess (*shouts*) Don't judge me! (*more quietly*) I see myself.

Nick I've got to get back, I don't like to leave Marisa on her own. I'm sorry.

Tess Please give her the letter. Please.

Robert Tess –

Tess Don't –

> *Nina and Hugh crowd on, followed by* **Victor**, *the social worker, and then April and Jamie.*

Nina You were wonderful.

Hugh It's our first evening out together.

Robert (*to Hugh and Nina*) How's the baby?

Hugh She's with our the tenth nanny. Nina says it's because I've bullied her into recording too soon.

Nina After all we've been through, I hardly see her.

Hugh But we're writing a song called 'How I Killed the Nannies'. That's off the record, Victor.

Nina This is Victor, our social worker, he's been coming for six months to see if I'm a fit mother, now he wants to meet our friends.

Victor I liked the play. I would have preferred a happy end.

April (*to Tess*) You look – ravaged. What's happened?

Tess La condition feminine – life.

Nina (*to Victor*) What are you writing?

Victor That your friends are multilingual and that's good for a transracial adoption.

Jamie Isn't she from Eastern Europe?

Victor We don't have many categories for adoption – she wasn't born here.

Robert (*to Nina*) I wish Tess and I had done what you've done.

Tess It's too late.

Nina I'd help you –

  Tess turns away.

Robert (*to Jamie*) How's the hospital?

Jamie Closed.

Robert Completely?

Jamie We fought. We lost. I've been offered another place, but that was my home. I may leave medicine altogether. My heart isn't in it.

Hugh (*to April*) How is Sappho?

Jamie I forgot to ask you.

April It's been rather popular.

Hugh And you're well?

April I live alone. I work. I have my students and my friends.

Nina Sounds like bliss.

April Yes, there's nothing to curtain me from the world the way a marriage, children, even a romance does. It makes me very clear-sighted.

Hugh And interesting.

April I think so, but no one talks about women like me. Particularly not in your magazines, Tess.

Tess I'd change that, but –

April We may not consume much, but we contribute a lot. We work. I think I live with dignity and some grace. I try to behave with decency. I feel lonely sometimes –

Nick I do too, but for different reasons ...

April But I keep going. My life is full. I want you to write a song about that, Nina, I want you to write a song about me.

Jamie I'd like a requiem for my hospital. For England.

Nina I've brought my child to this country, I have to believe in it.

Nick Victor, why are you wearing slippers?

Victor I wear them in the office, it's warmer and it saves on shoes. I had to leave in a hurry to get here, someone must have hidden my shoes. I'm sorry.

Robert It's the longest day. The sun rises so early up here.

I don't want to stay by myself. Let's wait for it, let's talk.

Nick I don't know. Marisa –

April It's only a few hours.

Nina I want to get back to my child, but I also want to stay.

Hugh That's how it's always going to be.

Tess I'll stay.

Nina (*to Victor*) What are you writing now?

Victor That your child is going to be brought up in a very intellectual environment, but that it's not necessarily a negative point.

Tess We only want to try and understand what's happened.

Robert You could even say that's hopeful.

  Fade.

The Songs

(OPENING NUMBER)

Ah Ah Aaaouh … Aaaouh …
Ba da yabada ba da yabada (*repeated*)

I don't want to sleep, I don't want to sleep,
Don't want to waste my time,
People to meet, appointments to keep,
Dragons to slay and mountains to climb.
The present is mine for the asking,
The future's a moment away,
Gotta get up, gonna tear it apart
Like a kid on Christmas day.

And now it belongs to me:
I'm gonna change the world.

Don't want to sleep, don't want to sleep,
Don't want to waste my time.

————

(BIRTHDAY SONG)

As year follows year
The world's gettting wiser,
You get wiser too.
My dear friend Tess
I wish you success
In everything you do.
You're forty, Tess,
But nevertheless
Happy birthday to you.

(SCANNING)

There's a kind of heat, a kind of glow,
And then you feel and then you know
She's there –
A kind of scent, a kind of bloom
The stillness in a crowded room,
She's there.

Voices echo everywhere,
Faces are a blur,
Search for the signal –
That's her.

There's a kind of heat, a kind of glow,
And then you feel and then you know
It's her –
A certain call, a certain voice
And then you fall, you have no choice –
It's her –
My little lost/found child.

———

(WAITING)

Time goes slowly when the world is waiting,
Hear the pulse that quickens then recedes,
Café tables, cigarettes and silence:
Waiting, waiting.

In the square the citizens are freezing,
In the dark the waiters come and go,
Hear the scream of emptiness and silence, endless
Waiting, waiting, waiting, waiting.

A girl at the gate, the end of day
And she has to wait until the car arrives.
There in the crowd there's that voice that is calling me
Loud and clear: I'm here to take you home.
Waving, desperately waving,
Waiting, waiting, waiting, waiting.